PEACE AND PURITY

PEACE
AND
PURITY

THE STORY OF THE BRAHMA KUMARIS
A SPIRITUAL REVOLUTION

LIZ HODGKINSON

Health Communications, Inc.
Deerfield Beach, Florida

www.hci-online.com

Library of Congress Cataloging-in-Publication Data

Hodgkinson, Liz.
  Peace & purity : the story of the Brahma Kumaris : a spiritual
revolution / Liz Hodgkinson.
    p. cm.
  ISBN 1-55874-962-4 (tp)
  1. Brahmakumari. 2. Spiritual life—Brahmakumari. I. Title:
Peace and purity. II. Title.

BL1274.24 .H63 2002
294.5'56—dc21   2001051783

©2002 The Brahma Kumaris
ISBN 1-55874-962-4

Publisher: Health Communications, Inc.
          3201 S.W. 15th Street
          Deerfield Beach, FL 33442-8190

Cover design by Krave Ltd., London UK.
Inside book design by Lawna Patterson Oldfield

CONTENTS

To Neville
who continues to be a
wonderful friend, ally and
walking companion.

ACKNOWLEDGMENTS

I should particularly like to thank Maureen Goodman, who unearthed much valuable archive material for me; Jaymini Patel, who has taken a keen interest in the project throughout; Jayanti Kirpalani for many long, informative and enjoyable sessions together; Nirwair Singh, who had the initial inspiration for the book; Jane Conway-Gordon, my agent, and Judith Kendra, publishing director at Rider, for their enthusiasm and positiveness.

PROLOGUE

It all seemed so typically Indian, even for those who had never been to India before. We arrived, a small group of bewildered, exhausted, bedraggled Westerners, at Ahmedabad airport in the middle of the night, to be jostled and hustled continuously by a seething throng of raggedly dressed men hopefully offering every tourist service imaginable: a taxi, accommodation, food, drink, sightseeing tours, snacks, carry your luggage, look after you, take you to good hotel, very cheap . . .

It was, in fact, every tourist's worst Indian nightmare: to be swooped on and hassled by hordes of dirty, unshaven men at a time when resistance was at an all-time low. But we were not tourists, exactly. We were delegates, on our way to a week-long Peace of Mind Retreat at Mount Abu, headquarters of the Brahma Kumaris World Spiritual University. And before long, representatives of this university, with long years of practice in fending off unwelcome vendors, came to our rescue.

The two white-clad BK brothers (both Westerners) who met us steered us straight towards a waiting Brahma Kumaris bus, and out of the way of the shouting, jostling, insistent vendors.

Brother David, a blond-haired British dentist who had become a BK more than two decades previously, opened up the luggage compartment of the bus and inside the darkness, something stirred. One of our number sprang back in alarm. "What was that?" they cried. "There's a creature at the back of the luggage compartment, I swear it! Or am I hallucinating?" We were all so exhausted, so dazed from lack of sleep and fifteen or more hours spent in continuous uncomfortable transit that we had difficulty in distinguishing dream from reality. But another traveller said: "Yes, something did move. I saw it too."

David, veteran of very many night trips to collect foreigners from Ahmedabad, laughed. "That's the luggage *wallah*," he explained, as the small creature of the night began to arrange huge amounts of luggage in the boot of the bus. We dimly wondered whether our luggage was actually on the bus—in all the chaos it seemed impossible—but at this stage we couldn't really care. All we wanted now was some sleep.

Within about five minutes of boarding the BK bus we were at their Ahmedabad Center which looked, even in the pitch black of the Indian night, gleaming and imposing and rather ornate in the Eastern style. It is a large new center, built specially to accommodate the ever-growing hordes of people who now jet in from all over the world to make their pilgrimage to Mount Abu.

Mount Abu is a good five hours' drive from Ahmedabad and,

although there has been talk for many years of constructing an airport on the mount, at the time of our visit this had not even begun to happen.

On sleepwalking out of the BK bus, we were assigned temporary rooms at the Ahmedabad Center in order to freshen up before making the onward journey by hired coach. We were requested to be outside the front door and ready, with our luggage, by eight sharp, so as it turned out there would be little chance of much sleep that night, as by the time we got out of the coach and reunited ourselves with our luggage (amazingly, every piece was on board) it was 5:00 A.M. already.

The Ahmedabad Center, staffed by young Indian women wearing white saris, bustles twenty-four hours a day with visitors from all over the world. Phones, faxes, e-mails, mobiles are kept constantly busy as sisters arrange flights, passports, visas, tickets and argue forcibly with Indian officials to make the impossible happen.

There were four of us altogether in our "freshen up" room: myself, two delegates from America, and Maureen, the wife of David the dentist and herself a dedicated Brahma Kumari. Maureen, a small, dark Liverpudlian, who is often mistaken for an Indian, was on her twenty-second trip to India, so it was all old hat to her. She unwound her white sari to have a (cold) shower in the bathroom, while the rest of us tried to put our heads down for an hour or two's nap before resuming our journey. Sleep though, was impossible, tired as we were: For one thing, the Ahmedabad Center was extremely noisy with bells and phones and loudspeakers constantly going (the BKs worship silence and after only a few minutes' experience of the non-stop cacophony of India, one can appreciate why), and for another, we were actually too exhausted to sleep. None of us could wind down enough.

So it was without great effort that we assembled on the steps of the center after breakfast, at 8:00 A.M. the next morning. By now, not only was it broad daylight, but all of Ahmedabad had woken up, and were letting us know it. Slim, brightly dressed women with bare midriffs swayed along with their red cotton skirts brushing the ground as they herded tiny donkeys, weighed down with panniers of sand, on to a building site. There they emptied the sackcloth panniers as the donkeys waited patiently to be taken to collect the next load—the construction industry in India! At the same time, cows, buffaloes, pigs, sheep, dogs wandered by themselves down the unmade-up road as cars, lorries and scooters, all madly hooting, swerved to avoid them.

It was a picturesque-enough scene, and those with enough energy or presence of mind to preserve it forever got out their cameras and camcorders and began snapping the local life being played out before them. It was all very filmic, but where, we dimly wondered, were our coaches? Aha, at ten past eight, on time for India, they trundled up. Good. Oh, no, spoke too soon. True, three smallish coaches—full-size ones can't negotiate the narrow and bendy track that winds perilously up to Mount Abu—turned into the road. But there they stayed, down at the bottom. We picked up our luggage to meet the coaches but the BK sisters supervising the event motioned us to put our cases down. Something was up. Something was wrong. A couple of sisters went up to the drivers of the coaches, and heated discussions, accompanied by wild arm and hand gestures and much head-nodding, ensued.

But no progress appeared to be made. The coach drivers got into some kind of furious argument with each other as we zonked-out travellers stood there continuing to take in the slow-moving, good-humored peasant life around us.

At last, at 10:00 A.M., only two hours after our scheduled departure time, the drivers' argument seemed to be settled and we thankfully clambered into the coaches. BK sisters and brothers brought on board bottles of mineral water, fruit and food for the journey. Our advance literature had warned us not to be tempted by any roadside food vendors, however delicious the food looked and smelled, "for your own good."

At ten past ten, having hooted the various animals and vehicles on the side street out of the way and made it out on to the main road, the coaches stopped again and the drivers got out for another argument. Then, after that was settled, each coach had to stop a few yards down the road to fill up with petrol, prompting the logical question from one of our number: "Why couldn't they have filled up *before* setting off, when the petrol station was only a few yards from the center?"

As with so many apparently logical questions, in India there was no easy answer to that, so the traveller sighed, shut his eyes and tried to go to sleep. But however tired, the constant honking of traffic—all vehicles in India sound their horns all the time—the bumps in the road, the lack of leg room in the coaches and general discomfort of the seats made any kind of sleep impossible. For most of us, that is. I glanced over at Maureen, the British-born BK, to find her deeply, blissfully, enviously, asleep. As a seasoned traveller in India, she could, it appeared, take it all perfectly in her stride.

A number of toilet stops were scheduled along the way, and these were an experience in themselves. The toilets, attached to hotels or restaurants, were not only filthy, but of the squatting type. Because of the difficulty in using them and the squeals of disgust, each fifteen-minute toilet stop took well over an hour, adding horribly to the length of the journey. Then the ascent of Mount Abu was not for the faint-hearted: hairpin bends, sheer drops on either side, lorries and coaches careering past us all made us wonder what on earth we had let ourselves in for. Throughout the journey we were ashen from fatigue and fear.

We were supposed to be at our destination by lunchtime. But because of the many delays, it was actually after 5:00 P.M. when the coaches eventually turned into the wide gates of Gyan Sarovar, or Academy for a Better World, our destination. By this stage we were beyond tiredness, beyond sleep, beyond even speaking. But we were not too exhausted to notice the utter, utter contrast between the chaos, dirt and disorganization of the India we had experienced so far, and this place.

It helped of course that the sun was still shining brightly in a cloudless sky, in complete contrast to the dreary, cold November we had left behind in London, and that the weather was warm. But Gyan Sarovar, the newest and in some ways most impressive of all Brahma Kumaris enterprises, was much like reaching a fairy-tale castle, a Garden of Eden, after untold horrors and privations on the way. On each side of the wide driveway was a landscaped garden bursting with trees, bushes, shrubs, flowers and potted plants in thousands of separate containers. The aspect was so pleasing, so welcoming, so well-designed, it looked as though some feng shui expert had been at work, as throughout most of India even large important buildings have a cluttered, higgledy-piggledy air.

But here, subtly lit fountains played in the middle of sparkling ornamental lakes. There were huge, life-size elephants, camels and kangaroos in topiary, rising out of the ground on firm big feet. The buildings themselves were modern, white and shining, built right into the rock. And it was all clean, so clean, with not even a blade of grass or leaf out of place. It was so, so—well, *unIndian*.

The inhabitants were all clean and shining too, the sisters dressed in white saris and the brothers in white kurta pajamas. Most looked Indian, but one or two—including my exhusband who was wearing a large badge which said Usher—were Western.

Could this really be India, we marvelled to each other, agreeing that the complex looked more like a prosperous little university campus in Florida than anything we had either seen so far, or imagined, in India. Gyan Sarovar—the term means Lake of Knowledge—is modern, efficient, built to a streamlined, logical plan, and it is state of the art, too, as it pioneered the use of solar panels in India for heating and electricity.

But although our initial impression of Gyan Sarovar was of a pastoral paradise, such as poets have described, with its fountains, thousands of trees, vines, flowers and rolling lawns and warm spring-like weather, this particular terrestrial heaven, as we were soon to learn, is a busy place, organizing conferences, seminars and tutorials all year round, for both Indians and foreigners.

Our group checked in, were assigned rooms and handed information packs in pale-blue plastic folders. Then we made our way to Harmony House, which was the main accommodation block, and discovered that the introductory session of the conference was to begin in only a few minutes, at six o'clock. So no sleep for a few more hours, we sighed.

Harmony House, though, was another pleasant discovery. At the end of a gentle slope, it has been especially designed to meet the needs of sophisticated, critical Westerners. As such, it is somewhere between a retreat and a modern university hall of residence. Most of the rooms are twin-bedded and all have shower rooms with Western flush toilets and basins. The rooms are simply furnished, with cheap fabrics and fittings—the university does not believe in unnecessary frills and fripperies—but are adequate and comfortable. By now completely on automatic pilot, I showered (the water was blissfully hot, thank goodness), changed from my dark travel clothes into more suitable white trousers and sweater, and made my way to the main auditorium, noticing a big sign outside the accommodation block informing guests they were to be fully dressed at all times when venturing out of their rooms, and that strict celibacy was to be observed. Perhaps not so much like a college hall of residence then after all!

The conference I had come to attend was called Peace of Mind—the Mount Abu Experience, and had been organized by the Australian branch of the BK for non-Indians.

Harmony Hall, the auditorium, seats 1,500, and has simultaneous translation facilities for about twenty different languages. These were needed immediately, as the 250 or so delegates at this conference came from around forty-five countries including the United Arab Emirates, Latvia, Vietnam, Japan, Brazil, China and Malaysia. At a quick glance, there seemed to be about twice as many women as men and the entire Japanese contingent, consisting of the tiniest grown-ups I have ever seen, was female.

The program started with a song, and then there was an introductory talk by Charlie Hogg, an amiable Aussie who had become a BK twenty-three years previously, when a wandering hippie and seeker. Now he is a middle-aged man running a thriving and innovative BK center in Australia. This was followed by a talk in English from Nirwair Singh, an urbane and stylish man from a Sikh background who has been a BK living at Mount Abu since 1963.

The final part of the program before dinner was a short talk in Hindi by Dadi Prakashmani, the worldwide administrative head of the organization. Dadi (the term means elder sister) joined the institution in the mid-1930s as a teenager, and has never known any other life. Her talk centered on the great need for peace in the world today, and ended with the thought that if a person has happiness, then they have every-thing. Without happiness, life has no meaning, and nothing else makes up for it.

After all the talks finished, we were invited to go up to Dadi and receive our gifts, which included a large woollen shawl, still in its polythene wrapping. These shawls were to become invaluable garments, we learned, in the week that lay ahead. It was cold in the early mornings and evenings, and shawls were the ideal wraparound warmers for this climate.

We paraded out of the auditorium and were shepherded into the vast self-service dining hall for dinner. The tables were large and square, each seating about eight people. The food was Indian vegetarian, although as a concession to the Westerners present there were mountains of chips (fries) and also bread and butter. There was water, tea or coffee to drink. No alcohol is allowed at this or any other BK center.

After dinner on this first night there were no more programs, so, at last, we could all go thankfully to bed. I was grateful that I had been assigned a room to myself—most people had to share—and it was not long before I fell into a profound and lengthy sleep. I even slept through the loudspeakers which awoke the faithful for four A.M. meditation the following morning.

The rest of the week followed a busy and productive schedule. There were talks, seminars, dances, dramas, visits to places of interest nearby, meditation sessions, question-and-answer sessions, group sessions, shopping trips and opportunities to share experiences. The Spiritual University, which has been in Mount Abu since the early 1950s, now has five separate complexes on the mountain, each impressive in its own way.

At its heart is Madhuban, the original site which is about half an hour's drive away from Gyan Sarovar. Madhuban, which grew up piecemeal as the institution gradually expanded, is much more "Indian" than the academy, with folksy little buildings, shrines, rooms that seem to become marginally darker when lit, and, at the best of times, flickering electricity and uncertain power supplies. But it has its own charm, and several delegates said that they preferred it, as it seemed so exotic and oriental. Most of the original members of the institution, those who joined in the mid-1930s, live in Madhuban, in simple, starkly furnished single rooms. They own no possessions apart from necessary personal items such as a watch or spectacles, and receive no money or salary from the institution for their work. Nirwair calls himself a "penniless prince" as, in common with other dedicated members, he has no money or goods of his own.

Halfway between Gyan Sarovar and Madhuban is the Global Hospital and Research Center, the only general hospital on Mount Abu, offering both the latest high-tech orthodox Western treatments and traditional Indian herbal treatments. The hospital has a psychiatric unit, a dental department, and a gynecology and obstetrics department. It also runs a village outreach program, where medicines and hospital services are taken to a number of the very poor, remote villages on Mount Abu.

The Peace Park, also owned and run by the university, is a wonderful, rather formally laid out large garden, somewhat like Kew Gardens in Britain, except that there is no admission charge.

Down at the bottom of Mount Abu is Taleti, a giant complex, more utilitarian than the academy, and built to accommodate very large numbers of people. The main hall there, Shantivan, can comfortably hold 10,000 people—and did, on one special night that I was there.

At one level, our retreat was organized much like a secular conference, with a varied program of events and activities. But there were a number of important differences. One was that nobody was making any money out of this particular event, nor were any of us charged anything. All we had to find were our air fares and transport to and from India. Thereafter, everything was taken care of by the Brahma Kumaris. There were no fees charged for either the conference or the accommodation, or for trips to local places of interest. Even the laundry facilities were free. We were invited to put our dirty clothes in a basket, and by next evening they were returned, beautifully washed and ironed.

In fact, the Brahma Kumaris never charge fees for any of their programs or events anywhere in the world. Yet nothing is cheapskate. All the delegates present agreed that this conference was in every way of the highest quality, and that our material as well as spiritual comforts were ideally met.

But the lack of commercialism was not the only unusual aspect of this international conference. For one thing, all the organizers were in a constant good mood. Everybody was smiling, cheerful and happy and, although extremely busy, never appeared hassled, fazed or frustrated. When asked how they managed to stay so serene, the reply was always: meditation. Regular meditation, in the early morning and evening, and at specific points during the day, reminded the organizers to stay calm and stress-free. And, certainly, it seemed to be an effective method of remaining positive.

The other striking aspect was that, although the week's program was packed with nonstop activities, there was a potent, almost tangible atmosphere of peace pervading the entire campus.

There seemed to be no ego, no arrogance, no jostling for position. At one question-and-answer session, one delegate asked a senior sister: "Do you believe in miracles?" The answer came that nowadays there are no miracles, no wondrous happenings, to which Paul Woolf, a senior lawyer from London, remarked: "This place is a true miracle."

Everybody agreed with Paul. At the end of the week all the delegates felt they had experienced something very unusual, very remarkable, even if they were not exactly sure at this point what they *had* experienced.

It very much reminded me of the prophecy in Isaiah, which states that all races will eventually come to the mountain of the Lord. The verses, from Isaiah 11: 2-5, were rendered into a hymn which was popular in my youth, but is most probably not much sung nowadays:

Behold the mountain of the Lord
In latter days shall rise
On mountain tops, above the hills
And draw the wondering eyes

To this, the joyful nations round
All tribes and tongues, shall flow
Up to the hill of God, they'll say
And to his house we'll go.

Most of the tribes and tongues, with the week's programs made intelligible by tireless simultaneous translators, went away with many questions ringing in their head. Just *how* do they do it? How can they erect such wonderful buildings, hold such impressive conferences, while not charging anybody? Where *does* all the money come from?

For the place cannot run on nothing. In the offices there were banks of computers and other high-tech equipment. The Spiritual University is fully online and much of its organization is now carried out via the Internet and e-mail.

There were many mobile phones in evidence. There were dozens of vehicles, from lorries or trucks and buses to limousines and vans and scooters. Each day they were cooking for several hundred people, and this number can go up to several thousand in busy seasons. The new buildings and complexes are architect-designed, and close attention has been paid to modern ideas of environment, recycling, irrigation and landscaping. The Global Hospital, though staffed by fully qualified doctors and nurses, offers much treatment free of charge.

To all the delegates on this retreat, the set-up seemed wondrous, unearthly, even impossible. So—who exactly are the Brahma Kumaris, and what is their secret?

ONE

EARLY DAYS

Even the most unobservant of visitors to Harmony Hall in Gyan Sarovar would not be able to miss noticing an extremely large, not to say vast, picture of an elderly Indian gentleman in the main auditorium. At least twenty feet long by eight feet high, this disembodied face wreathed in celestial light looks out to all from the back of the stage. There are also pictures of this same man in every bedroom in the residential block, Harmony House.

His face further appears on the back of exercise books, on keyrings and many other artifacts, and in every meditation and public room. He even has his own room, Baba's room, in each of the Mount Abu complexes. These rooms are shrouded floor to ceiling in draped white fabric, and have the atmosphere of a holy shrine.

So who is this man, then? Some kind of guru? Clearly, he is seen as somebody of supreme importance to the Brahma Kumaris organization.

He is, in fact, Brahma Baba, the founder of the movement who died, or "left the body," on January 18, 1969, at the age of ninety-three, very many years before any Western centers or impressive buildings or programs had come into being. He is greatly respected and remembered, but he is, all BKs will tell you, most emphatically not a guru.

From the very start of their movement, the BKs have rejected the notion of a guru, as this implies worship of a human being, and they do not consider it appropriate that a mere human, however enlightened or praiseworthy he or she might be, deserves this kind of adulation. Praise, worship and remembrance should be reserved, they consider, for God, the ever-incorporeal being, and nobody else.

Thus Brahma Baba, in spite of the many images of his face everywhere, is not worshipped as a guru. In fact, he is not worshipped at all. The huge, and to Western perceptions maybe somewhat kitsch, representations of this man all over the Mount Abu centers are merely to remind everybody, both dedicated BKs and casual visitors, of the person whose initial vision and courage began this organization which is today so confident, prosperous and well regarded.

It is perhaps because the BKs have always rejected the very concept of human gurus that Brahma Baba's name is still little known outside India. This is in dramatic contrast to the names of, say, Sai Baba, Bhagwan Shree Rajneesh (later known as Osho) and Maharishi Mahesh Yogi: Indian gurus who have become famous in the West. During his lifetime,

Brahma Baba himself rejected any worship or adulation and kept an extremely low profile. He was so averse to personal publicity that he would even get off at a railway station before the one scheduled if he thought there might be a reception committee and garlands to meet him. Unlike many Eastern gurus who go out of their way to court publicity and fame, Brahma Baba was always determined to remain as incognito as possible.

So who was this man, and how was the movement started? The story begins in the early 1930s, in Hyderabad, Sind, where there lived a group of closely interconnected, interrelated and intermarried families known as the Bhaibund community. This community was wealthy, influential, and had for many years devoted itself to prospering in business.

Nominally orthodox Hindus, the Bhaibunds had, by all accounts, become extremely degenerate by the 1930s. Their once-strict standards of behavior had deteriorated badly and most of them were now eating meat, smoking cigarettes and drinking alcohol, copying the Westerners with whom many of them now traded, but all expressly forbidden by their religion. They had also become dishonest and fraudulent in their business dealings, and were living lives of empty ostentation and show, each competing to outdo the other in status and position. One contemporary commentator remarked: "While outwardly they flourished, inside they became ever greedier, dishonest and lustful."

Brahma Baba, or Lekhraj Khubchand Kirpalani, as he was known in those days, was a member of this community. Coming from relatively humble beginnings—his father was the local schoolteacher—Dada Lekhraj had risen by his own efforts to become one of the richest men in India, through dealing in diamonds and precious stones. His company was based in Calcutta, and his main business was in supplying diamonds and jewels to many royal families.

However, by the early 1930s, when he was in his mid-fifties, he was becoming increasingly interested in searching for truth, and began to have a horror of trading for profit. This feeling eventually became so strong that in 1936 he decided to take early retirement and sell up his business. He would trade no more. Of course as he was already enormously wealthy, he could afford to indulge these feelings.

But it was not just the modern way of doing business, where profit and money-making were worshipped above all else that made him sad. He was also becoming disgusted with the manners and morals of his own community. The greed and fraudulent business practices that had become a standard way of life were bad enough, but by far the worst scandal, as Dada Lekhraj came to see it, was in the treatment of the community's women. Denied an education, profession or money of their own, the only reason for a woman's existence was to become somebody's wife, through an arranged marriage, and thereafter a brood mare. It was the custom for a girl upon marriage to go and live at her father-in-law's house, where-after she led an existence of almost total imprisonment and subservience. She had no rights, no say, no choices.

Most middle- and upper-class Hindu women in those days wore veils and, whether married or not, were not allowed outside the four walls of their father's or husband's home without express permission. There was no possibility of divorce, no opportunity to enter any profession, or to become a religious renunciate even, an honorable path open to Eastern men (and men only) since ancient times. "For them," writes BK Jagdish Chander in *Adi Dev*, his book about Brahma Baba, "there was no escape from the life sentence of marriage."

That "life sentence" also included sex on demand, as no woman ever dare refuse her husband his conjugal rights. A husband, however vicious, brutal or stupid he might be, was seen as his wife's guru, her god, and as such a perfect being. If he died and she was left a widow, she had to put on perpetual mourning, and be reduced in the household to the status of servant.

As with animals, it was a matter of chance and luck as to whether a woman ended up with a good master. Some husbands were brutal and violent—this kind of behavior even being encouraged and applauded among husbands—and there was no redress at all. There were no refuges or shelters for battered women to go to, and few married women, however badly treated, would ever go back to their own father's house, as to do so would be to lose face in the community. Hindu women were taught to tolerate, tolerate and tolerate— and then tolerate some more.

Some women, undoubtedly, did have good husbands, and not all arranged marriages were unhappy. But on marriage a woman was, almost literally, sold into slavery. Worse, the existence of the dowry system meant that a potential husband had to be persuaded with the offer of a large sum of money to take this low-grade creature, a female, as his wife. The feminist novelist Virginia Woolf observed at about the same time that in Britain, every woman became "the slave of any boy whose parents force a ring on her finger."

But at least in the England of the 1930s women were enfranchised (just), they were allowed a university education and entrance to some professions. The women's rights movement had begun, however shakily. But the India of the 1930s, although still under British rule, did not have even the first faint stirrings toward any kind of equality or independence for women. The young waif-like Indira Nehru, later Prime Minister Mrs. Gandhi, was attending Oxford University in the 1930s, but that was a rare privilege reserved for the very top of the elite. Also, Jawaharlal Nehru, Indira's father and India's first prime minister, was a revolutionary and intellectual who adored and wanted the very best for his only child.

Very few Indian women of the time had even a primary, let alone a university, education.

In the Bhaibund community and, for that matter, throughout India, men ruled women absolutely. As Dada Lekhraj now came to see it, that would perhaps not matter quite so much if the men were selfless, honest, admirable people, worthy of total worship and adoration from their women. But the problem was, they were not. Far from it. They were full of every kind of vice and corruption. Yet these flawed creatures were placed wholly and totally in charge of women. From any logical and humane standpoint, this could not be right. After all, women were human beings too, reasoned Dada: quite a revolutionary concept in itself for the time.

But what, he wondered, *could one do about it?* Custom and tradition were very strong, so strong, in fact, that although the British had ruled India for more than two centuries, they had not been able to make even the tiniest difference to the centuries-old custom of trading young boys and girls in marriage, without giving the couple any say as to whether they themselves wanted to embark on such an intimate and permanent arrangement. Dada Lekhraj had himself married two daughters in this manner. One was given at the age of fifteen to a man of fifty.

Dada had also himself, he now realized, been guilty of offering his flesh and blood for social position and according to mindless tradition. So, how could the once-high standards of the community be brought back, and how could the position of women be improved so that they had dignity, self-esteem and independence? The women themselves were unlikely to rebel or fight for themselves, as they were socialized to be timid, fearful, passive. Also, as they had no money or means of earning any, escape was totally impossible. Dada Lekhraj felt that trying to change laws would not help either, as the customs were so embedded, baked as it were, into the very way of life.

Nor was it, he felt, any use going to the spiritual teachers because although they were supposed to be founts of wisdom, in fact they had become as greedy and corrupt as the rest of the male population. It eventually came to Dada after deep contemplation of these issues and the problems that reform presented, that deep, lasting social change had to be brought about by some other, vastly more effective means.

It also came to him that he himself would have to be the instrument for social change, as he, and nobody else, it seemed, had been troubled by these thoughts. Luckily, he had something, or at least, some*one*, extremely influential on his side, and this was God himself. As time went on, Dada became ever more certain that God was calling him, a businessman and diamond merchant (retired), to undertake work of the greatest importance, God's work no less, to reform society.

Throughout the ages many reformers, particularly those who have made a lasting impact on the world, have become convinced that they have heard the voice of God speaking directly to them. In Judaism we are told that God spoke through the prophets; in Christianity through John the Baptist and Jesus Christ, and, in somewhat less exalted spheres, Joan of Arc and Florence Nightingale were both certain that God was calling them to do work they would never have considered, or had the courage to do, on their own.

It has often happened that when an ordinary-seeming man or woman is singled out to do great things they have visions, hear voices, or see future scenes played out before them, before it becomes clear what they must do. Sometimes angels come and whisper in their ear, as with the Virgin Mary and the angel Gabriel.

Whether, in our secular, scientific age, we believe that these voices, visions and angels are actually heavenly visitations or the product of a fevered imagination is not really the point. They are certainly real enough for the recipient, and in some cases so vivid, so insistent, that the visionary has no choice but to act on them. And if the eventual result is to benefit humanity, who is to deny their reality or impact?

And now, all this began to happen to Dada Lekhraj. Although he had not been of a noticeably visionary or poetic turn of mind in the past, he now began to have dramatic visions experienced through altered states of consciousness. At first these visions were of divine bliss and ecstasy, heavenly visions, but, as time went on, they became more disturbing.

In later visions Dada began to see bombs being manufactured and fired, and whole cities being blown up in an instant. He saw gigantic fireballs, cities in flame, continents being destroyed.

At the time, as several BK commentators have pointed out, atomic bombs had not even been invented. But there was more: Dada also saw in his visions cities, countries, continents being destroyed by environmental pollution, by earthquakes, freak weather conditions. He came to realize that he was witnessing a similar state of destruction to what had been described in ancient scriptures.

As Dada had always been so level-headed, so practical, before, his friends and family wondered whether he had become slightly unhinged when he tried to describe what he had seen during his meditation sessions. First he was seeing heaven, then he was seeing hell, as it seemed. He must be ill, they thought, maybe suffering from schizophrenia.

But whatever the explanation, the impact of these visions was powerful enough to have the effect of changing Dada's life for ever. His horoscope had foretold that he would not live beyond the age of sixty; now, nearing that time, he offered his body and his worldly wealth to God, and himself as a vehicle and vessel for godly work. All his previous desire for worldly wealth fell away and instead, he began to hold *satsangs*, or religious meetings, at his house in Hyderabad.

At first, these meetings were informal and held purely for members of his own family. But gradually, as the word spread round the community that something special happened at these gatherings, ever more people came. Within three years, 500 members of the Bhaibund community were attending regular satsangs at Dada's house, and because of the increasing numbers, a more formal structure was soon needed. The burgeoning movement became known as the Om Mandali, or the gathering of Om.

Most, although not all, of the original members of the Mandali were women. Tied to house and husband, women of that time had few social outlets, but there was one thing they were allowed to do, and that was to attend satsangs, harmless religious gatherings at which people would chant the name of God and perhaps hear a discourse on some aspect of the scriptures. Men allowed their women to undertake this activity as it gave them something to do and kept them out of mischief. The men, meanwhile, were often away on business. In fact by this time, the great majority of the male members of the Bhaibund community were away on business for most of the year.

Children also started to attend these meetings. Most Indian children, in common with children in the West, are bored by religious or spiritual gatherings, and fidget and wriggle all the time. Yet at the Om Mandali young children not only sat in complete silence, they actually clamored to go.

The meetings were particularly attracting young teenage girls, one of whom was fifteen-year-old Rama, now Dr. Dadi Prakashmani, administrative head of the Brahma Kumaris worldwide.

Dadi remembers the impact of those early days:

One day I had an extraordinary dream, where I saw a beautiful garden with Krishna and the angel Brahma. Then a classmate at school invited me along to Baba's satsang, saying that there is one Dada who chants Om. My parents gave me permission to go—Baba always insisted on written permission from parents if you were a minor—and the first time I went there I saw the same angel Brahma as in the dream. The angel form full of light attracted me, and I had to stay.

Other children and teenagers were having similar experiences. Dadi Gulzar, now in charge of the Delhi centers, was eight years old when she first started attending the satsangs. She says:

I was with an uncle and aunt at a satsang one evening, when I saw a scene of Krishna at eight years old, the same age as myself. It seemed so real and not like a dream. At the time, I knew nothing of visions or trances, and it seemed as if I was seeing it in fact, rather than in my mind. It is so vivid, even now, that I can remember every detail more than sixty years later. I seemed to be sitting in a hall decorated with bells, and the whole room was lit with sparkling diamonds. In the end I started crying, and the grown-ups around me asked: "Where did you go, what happened to you?" They then showed me devotional pictures, pictures of Krishna and asked whether this was what I saw. But the pictures were pale imitations, nothing like the real thing as I had seen it in my vision.

Dadi Lachu, or Lakshmi, a tiny person of no more than four foot ten, has been a Brahma Kumari since the age of six, when she began attending Dada's satsangs with her mother, sisters and brothers. She describes how the meetings struck her then:

We all used to sit and chant. I was one of six children, and we all enjoyed it very much. Several of the children used to go into trance, and none of us was ever bored. At first, there were just five families who attended the satsangs Baba began holding at his large home in Hyderabad. There seemed to be such a special atmosphere then. Baba himself would go into trance sometimes, and appeared to the gathering as Krishna. Those who attended the gathering felt that something very holy, something very wonderful, was taking place.

One particular teenage girl, a cousin of Dada Lekhraj's wife Jashoda, also began to attend the satsangs, and she seemed to be so special that before long she was put in charge of the entire operation, and Dada Lekhraj began to take a back seat. This girl's name was Radha, and she became known as Om Radhe. Eighteen years old when she began to attend the satsangs, by her early twenties she had renounced the possibility of any other kind of life to become the president of the Om Mandali.

Om Radhe was the classmate of Dadi Prakashmani, who was instrumental in persuading Om Radhe to attend in the first place. Although so young, Om Radhe seemed to have natural qualities of leadership and power, and she soon became the public face and spokeswoman of the institution.

As more girls began to come, Dada set up a trust whereby all his wealth passed into the hands of the young women dedicating themselves to the fledgling organization. He also drew up a constitution which said that the Om Mandali would always be run by women, never men.

Now, the lives of those who attended the satsang on a daily basis took on a new meaning and purpose. The meetings would begin with the chanting of Om, then Baba, as he was now called, would read a chapter of the Bhagavad Gita on aspects of godly knowledge, then explain this to the gathering. After that, there would be a talk on the topic of the day, which might be the laws of karma, consciousness, good behavior, qualities of God, or the dawn of the new era. Those who came and listened were quite sure that, during these times, the presence of God Shiva, the Supreme Soul, quite literally entered the body of Baba.

Gradually the mainly young female members of the Mandali felt themselves imbued with unprecedented strength and resolve. They began to be self-determining, to lose their fear and terror of men, and to have genuine self-esteem. In fact, the Om Mandali gave assertiveness and con-sciousness-raising training to young women long before these concepts even existed in the West. And all the time, accord-ing to accounts of the time, the members were in a state of bliss and ecstasy, not anger and resentment, as was the case with many early Western feminists. The atmosphere at the meetings was most likely much more like that of the early Christians, where previously timid, passive women became strong and courageous, and ended up saints and martyrs, thrown to the lions for their unshakeable faith.

Also, the women attending the satsang regularly began to change their dress. Instead of richly colored clothes and jewels, artifacts proclaiming the wealth of their husbands or fathers, they now wore only simple white cotton clothes. White cotton was in those days considered a very low-grade fabric, worn only by the poor or by widows with no status in society. Their new form of dress was certainly not considered suitable wear for the wives or daughters of rich businessmen. Baba too gave up wearing his tailored Western suits, substituting these with simple white cotton *kurta* and *dhoti* such as coolies and peasants wear.

Soon there were so many children coming that Baba decided to open a boarding school. This was known as Om Nivas, and was run on strict, well-disciplined lines which included set hours for meditation, schoolwork and play. Visitors to the school remarked on how clean, tidy and well-behaved the children were.

In these ways, the Om Mandali grew and flourished undisturbed for two years. The school was established and running well. The organization was very wealthy, thanks to the funds provided by Baba, and so there was no need for fees or outside contributions.

All very nice. But major trouble was looming. The young girls and teenagers attending the Om Mandali were starting to express their distaste for marriage, for the very institution of holy wedlock, and were refusing to consider marriage themselves. Like Catholic nuns, they felt they had become married to God, and could not now contemplate the prospect of a secular husband. Then, three married women who had been attending Baba's satsang regularly actually refused to have sexual relations with their husbands. The husbands in question had been away for several months on business and, when they returned, demanded instant resumption of their marital rights.

When these were refused, the husbands flew into a rage. Whatever rubbish was Baba filling their wives' heads with? Before going to the satsang they would never have dared refuse. For their part, the women complained that their husbands were brutal, callous bullies and that they would not go back to them under any circumstances. Also, they had now been hearing on a daily basis that physical sex was impure, lustful, and that if they wanted to lead a genuinely spiritual life they should not consider marriage or allow themselves to be used as objects to satisfy the sexual lust of another.

Inevitably, word began to get around that the women attending Dada Lekhraj's satsang were refusing to consider physical sex, and eventually a popular newspaper, *The Illustrated Weekly of India,* sent a reporter to investigate the sensational rumors that women were making a unilateral decision to abstain from sex, whether married or not. The introduction to the story, published on July 13, 1938, and headlined Sind's celibate wives: Truth about the Hyderabad 'Strike,' read:

A delicate problem for a number of husbands in Hyderabad (Sind) has been set by their wives who have joined a new religious cult and taken vows of celibacy. They have informed their husbands that they are at liberty to take other wives. The families concerned belong mainly to the Bhaibund community and the panchayat [local court] has received a number of applications from husbands seeking permission to remarry. We asked a correspondent to go to Hyderabad to gather the facts and in the following article he explains what has happened.

Thousands of people in various parts of India who have read more or less garbled accounts of sensational happenings in Hyderabad (Sind) are asking themselves what is this Om

Mandali? Is it a new cult of self-restraint and "self-realization" with Mr. Lekhraj Khubchand as a genuine "Seeker after Truth"?

The movement started early this year in Hyderabad, the second largest town in Sind, but it only came into prominence about the middle of June when rumours about the implications of the new cult began to be noised abroad.

In Hyderabad Only

While Hyderabad is seething with excitement, comparatively little is heard in Karachi, nor are even the Hindus much concerned.

The reason for this apathy is not far to seek, for the movement is mainly confined to members of the Bhaibund community, young women supplying most of the recruits.

Brahmacharya, or celibacy, is the main principle of the movement. The women followers of Mr. Lekhraj Khubchand style themselves gopis, or nuns, and have taken vows of celibacy.

As far as the unmarried women are concerned these vows affect nobody but themselves, but with regard to the married women the case is very different. The husbands of the latter class have something to say and they are saying it in no uncertain terms. They believe that the behaviour of their wives is against all the tenets of Hindu law and is contrary to the laws of nature.

WIVES AS MATCHMAKERS

The wives agree that a great hardship is entailed and suggest a remedy—remarriage. Some of the young women are becoming matchmakers on behalf of their husbands and are going round looking for suitable girls to relieve them of a burden which they say they are no longer in a position to carry themselves.

Matters came to a climax towards the latter end of June when a number of aggrieved husbands and their friends met and marched to the two meeting places of the new religion.

A serious breach of the peace was only averted by the timely arrival of responsible officials and a strong police force.

PANCHAYAT CONSULTED

The Bhaibund panchayat were approached by some of the husbands who demanded early permission to remarry. Realizing the seriousness of the position the panchayat very wisely appointed a special committee of several respectable members of the Bhaibund community with Mr. Mangharam as president.

Prolonged sessions were held by the committee and evidence from all sides was carefully sifted.

This evidence was very similar, the husbands bringing forward overwhelming proof that their wives, under the influence of the teachings of Mr. Khubchand, were determined to keep their vows.

The ultimate findings of the committee were that the new cult was not in accord with the teachings of the Hindu religion and they therefore recommended that the meeting places should be closed down immediately. This was eventually done and the buildings are under police guard throughout the twenty-four hours.

MR. LEKHRAJ

Bhai Lekhraj has many supporters in Karachi where he is at present in residence. These people assert that he is a much-maligned man. They consider his teachings are those of a saint and that only by following his simple rules can "Eternal Life" be attained.

In appearance, Mr. Lekhraj is elderly, though well-preserved and his features have the stamp not only of the ascetic but the intellectual.

We can easily discount, therefore, the stories attributing a misuse of hypnotic powers over neurotic young women. It may be that the repercussions of his teachings were not of his own seeking nor is evidence readily available that he has actually induced married women to renounce their conjugal ties.

Be this as it may, the cult will not be suppressed in a day, while on the other hand the wide publicity given to the Hyderabad happenings may be conducive to a spread of the movement not only in Sind but to other parts of India.

Although the reporter did not manage to get any direct quotes, which would be considered essential for a story of such impact nowadays, the report gives what appears to be a pretty accurate and fair-minded rendering of the extremely complicated situation at that time. What the report does not say is that the "Mr. Mangharam" who headed the special committee appointed by the panchayat was none other than Dada Lekhraj's daughter's father-in-law.

Although dissatisfaction among the men denied conjugal rights had been growing for some time, matters came to a dramatic head when one of Baba's daughters returned to her parents' house after her husband went abroad, saying she was finding it impossible to live with her in-laws any more. Baba had married this particular daughter to the son of the Mukhi, one of the most politically influential and wealthy men in the city.

It had been considered at the time an advantageous match on both sides and, for a time, Baba's daughter was as happy as a young woman in her confined position could expect to be. She had gone from one wealthy household to another, and from her earliest years had been pampered and indulged. But now, her father began to feel he had himself done wrong in marrying his daughter at all, tying her down to perpetual sexual intercourse whether she wanted it or not, and without giving her any choice in the matter.

Word had got around the community that celibacy was being preached to unmarried women, and that married ones were being urged not to submit to the sexual demands of their husbands. It began to be rumored that the main aim of the Om Mandali was to abolish marriage and "normal relations" (in other words, utter subservience). Also, a rumor had been started that Baba had inveigled these young innocent girls to his house for his own nefarious reasons. These were the rumors that the newspaper reporter had been sent to investigate.

When Baba's daughter refused to go back to her husband on any account, the husband began alleging that Dada Lekhraj was inculcating notions of disobedience among married women. Baba was prevailed upon to make the women resume sexual relations with their husbands, but he refused, saying that he had no right to do this, and that cruelty and maltreatment were behind the women's decisions.

There has, of course, always been a tradition of celibacy in Hinduism, but it was understood that this was a decision only men could make, as only males had such powers of discrimination. Many years previously, Mahatma Gandhi had proclaimed eternal celibacy for himself, maintaining that sex drained him of energy needed to continue his campaign for Indian independence. Men could become celibates if they felt a spiritual calling, but women were not allowed to decide such a matter for themselves. These decisions were particularly not welcomed in such a tradition-bound community as the Bhaibund, where the look of the thing was of supreme importance.

There was another factor to these female declarations of celibacy and that was that if wives refused sex it would be hard for their menfolk to find physical satisfaction elsewhere. There was virtually no such thing as adultery as women in the community, both married and single, were so closely guarded. And it was not acceptable for a strict Hindu to visit a prostitute, although there were also rumors at the time that many of the men who spent so much of their time away on business were secretly keeping mistresses. But even if this was so in some cases, it would never do for your wife to refuse to have sexual intercourse with you. Even nowadays in the West, any suggestion of celibacy among married couples is greeted with sensational headlines—so one can only guess at the impact the Om Mandali was making in this regard.

This no-sex decision, which was understood to be a permanent one by the women, struck terror into the hearts of the men, who began to fear they would never have sex again if this situation continued. Nor would they have any bargaining power when it came to marrying their daughters. In fact their daughters, valuable trading assets, would be lost to them forever if they refused to marry.

The upshot was, as reported in the press, that Baba's daughter's father-in-law, Mukhi Mangharam, and a number of other aggrieved husbands and relatives formed what came to be called the Anti Om Mandali Committee, with the intention of having the institution closed down, and Baba discredited.

The Anti Committee was formed on June 21, 1938, and from then on the institution was under siege. The committee used any and every tactic at their disposal, from round-the-clock picketing and throwing stones and brickbats at the institution to trying to set fire to the buildings. The Mandali applied to the District Magistrate of the city for help and protection against the pickets, but he appeared to be on the side of the Anti Committee, and refused to take any action.

Om Radhe states in her account of the affair, *Is This Justice?*, that "nothing wrongful" was ever suggested by the British officials against the Mandali. It is most likely that they were at a complete loss to understand what was going on, as the once close-knit and peaceable community now seemed divided against itself.

Soon after the newspaper report appeared, things turned

very nasty indeed. Some parents, influenced or maybe intimidated by the Anti Committee, began to prevent their children from attending the school. Also, some children were forcibly dragged away from the school as rumors that Baba was practicing hypnotism and indulging in immoral practices intensified. One witness stated in a court case, of which there were many over the next few years, that he had seen Dada Lekhraj rubbing his hand against a girl's thigh. The Anti Committee said in a written statement, when the matter first came to court:

> It is not possible to say whether the satisfaction of his lust was the intention with which he originated these institutions Om Mandali and Om Nivas, but we are definitely of the opinion that at a very early stage, this became the main intention of Dada Lekhraj.

Dadi Manoharindra, now Director of the Raja Yoga Camps and administrator of Gyan Sarovar, was twelve years old when she first started attending Baba's satsangs. Then known as Hari, she describes the treatment she received from her family for daring to attend:

> The house where my family lived in Hyderabad was opposite Baba's, and I had been in the habit anyway of visiting his family. The satsangs began with chanting, and when the chanting ended I experienced such blissful silence and my consciousness began to change. I don't remember being bored at all, even though I was so young, and I began to experience myself as a peaceful being. My parents were not

interested themselves in the meetings, and when the Anti Committee was formed they refused to allow me to continue going. People told my parents that if I continued to attend the Mandali I would leave them and never return. So, to prevent me from going, they locked me up.

I told my parents that I was never going to get married. At this announcement, my father tortured me, slapped me and beat me and pulled my hair out in his rage. I told them that I did not want to marry an impure person, and that as I was already married to God, I did not want or need an earthly husband.

It is Indian custom of course that all daughters should get married, and there is no exception to this. My mother became furious, kept pushing me down and saying that these people were mesmerists, and had worked magic on me. They forced me to eat pig's meat to drive out the magic, forcing it down my throat. All Indian children are taught to respect their parents, no matter what, and Baba told me to continue to respect mine, as they did not understand what they were doing. Although I was kept locked up, every now and again I managed to escape and go to the Mandali. When my parents realized I was missing, they came and pulled me out of the gathering. I was not allowed to go, but I kept disobeying my parents and going. Such behavior was unthinkable on the part of children, and particularly for girls, who never opposed their parents in any way, but grew up timid little mice. But I could not keep away, young as I was, and even though I was tortured and punished for going.

Eventually, bowing to intense pressure from the Anti

Committee, the Sind government charged five members of the Mandali, one of whom was Baba, with disturbing the peace under Section 112 of the Criminal Procedure Code. Under this code, the Mandali was discredited and outlawed. The five people, three of whom were women, were bound over to keep the peace for six months and restrained from holding satsangs or meetings consisting of males and females. If allowed to continue, the Mandali had to be a gathering for ladies only.

The Mandali immediately appealed against this unjust decision, arguing that it was the Anti Committee, not themselves, who had been disturbing the peace by picketing, trying to burn down the buildings, forcibly preventing people from entering, and holding public processions and marches to protest against the Mandali. All letters to the authorities were signed by Om Radhe, not Baba. For much of this time Baba was in Karachi, distancing himself from affairs, and preparing himself spiritually for the even worse storms he felt certain lay ahead.

The Om Mandali case came to the High Court in Karachi on November 21, 1938, after attracting widespread media attention. Many articles and reports, both in favor of and against the Mandali, appeared in the local papers. The application, before the Hon. Mr Godfrey Davis and the Hon. Mr Eric Weston (both British judges) was to "quash proceedings pending an order passed by the City and Sub-Divisional Magistrate, Hyderabad, under Section 112 of the Criminal Procedure Code."

After hearing both sides, Godfrey Davis, the Judicial Commissioner of Sind and Eric Weston, Judge, set aside the order and quashed the proceedings. After this, the Om Mandali decided it would be better to move to Karachi permanently and give up the premises in Hyderabad. They now had permission to continue the Om Mandali, and felt that going to Karachi might give them a new and more peaceful start.

But they were wrong. Fifteen women who had been forcibly prevented from following the Mandali to Karachi decided that life was unbearable without Baba's satsangs and somehow found a means to go anyway. For the Anti party, writes Jagdish Chander in *Adi Dev*, "This was the last straw. They were determined to put an end to God's work." It could be said that a community that traded its sons and daughters like cattle was hardly likely to have empathy with anybody opposing its views. And, as the poet Shelley wrote: "If woman is a slave, can man be free?" The Bhaibund community had long lost its humanity—which was a major reason for the Om Mandali coming into existence in the first place.

Hari was one of the young women who defied her family and went to join Baba at Karachi.

Although still locked up, I managed to escape and I used my pocket money to get to Karachi. When my mother discovered I was missing, she went frantic, as she could not find me anywhere. A few days later, my mother came to see me in a taxi, with other family members. They all sat in a little room, and when I asked if they would like anything to eat or drink, they kidnapped me and bundled me into the taxi. Then they drove back to Hyderabad, saying I was never to go to the Om Mandali ever again.

I was completely miserable and kept telling my parents I wanted to go back. I asked them to give me permission in writing to go, but they refused. Even so, I went again, this time by bus. There was a bad accident on the way, which got into all the local papers, and my name appeared in the papers. Again, my mother came to Karachi and forced me home.

The official version of this story is that on January 18, 1939, Hari's mother and the mother of another girl who had escaped to Karachi filed an application in the Court of the Additional Magistrate in Karachi stating that their daughters, aged thirteen and twelve, had been induced to go to Karachi from Hyderabad and were being wrongfully detained at the Om Mandali. The court-ordered search warrants for the production of the minors Ganga and Hari, and this was carried out. The magistrate then ordered the girls to be kept in the custody of their mothers. Om Radhe appealed against the decision in the High Court, but on this occasion the magistrate's decision was upheld, as the girls in question were minors, and the court could not go against the parents. The judges, though, held that the magistrate was wrong in the order he passed.

Eventually, Hari's parents were persuaded to let their daughter stay at the Om Mandali—where she has been ever since.

In another important lawsuit, a husband sued for restitution of his conjugal rights. In this case, the British judge ruled that as the woman was a major—over eighteen years old—she could exercise her own choice in this matter. This judgment was extremely enlightened for the time, as in England wives were still legally the property of their husbands, and where conjugal rights were willfully refused the marriage could be annulled. There was also, in English law, no such thing as rape in marriage until the late 1980s. And although the British provided more of a presence than a repressive alien occupation, English law prevailed at that time in India, and High Courts were staffed by English lawyers.

But all was not over yet. The Om Mandali issue had divided the Sind government, and certain Hindu members of parliament threatened to resign unless the Om Mandali was finally outlawed. In fact, some walked into the parliament building with guns in their hands, threatening to use them unless the Mandali was instantly outlawed.

The government now played for time by appointing a fact-finding tribunal, which meant that Om Radhe and the other sisters running the institution had to have a crash course in legal matters.

On being ordered to "show cause" why the Mandali should not be outlawed, they painstakingly gathered evidence and affidavits which they felt proved that the institution was a peaceful organization working for good. But these were not heard or taken into account, and the upshot was that the tribunal, consisting mainly of friends and supporters of the Anti party, issued an *ex parte* decision that members of the Om Mandali should no longer be allowed to stay together, but must separate, and be outlawed as a dangerous institution.

The decision was reported in all the local papers, and caused an almighty media uproar. As Jagdish writes: "It was indeed a strange decision not merely because the members of the Om Mandali were like one large and close-knit family . . . but because Om Mandali was actually composed of whole

clans as well as unattached individuals. Should these house-
holds be forced to scatter?"

The action taken by the government filled very many
column inches in newspapers, with most reports expressing
outrage and bewilderment at its high-handed and totally
unfair decision.

Calling it an "All-India Issue," the *Daily Gazette's* article
on the matter on Tuesday, May 16, 1939 said:

> *In this particular matter the Sind government are propos-*
> *ing to tread underfoot no less a birthright of the Indian*
> *people than the civil liberties to which they are entitled*
> *under British rule . . . From the very start, the Allahbux*
> *Ministry have made a muddle of the Om Mandali problem,*
> *and now they wish to make confusion worse confounded . . .*
> *We are not concerned with the fate of Dada Lekhraj or Om*
> *Radhe; but we are concerned with the liberty which the Sind*
> *government propose to take with the civil liberty of the*
> *Indian people. Not only this province but the whole country*
> *expects the Sind government not to abuse the powers vested*
> *in it by the new constitution by taking any step which is*
> *opposed to reason and common sense.*

On Sunday June 4 the *Gazette* stated in another article:

> *We have made it abundantly clear that we do not hold*
> *any brief for Dada Lekhraj, nor have we upheld his teach-*
> *ings and his media of imparting them. But we feel it our*
> *bounden duty to enter an emphatic protest against the most*
> *dangerous step which the Sind government have taken,*

inasmuch as it tramples underfoot those civil liberties which are the birthright of every British subject . . . The Om Mandali issue was a purely social one, fought on both sides as a social question concerning the welfare of the Bhaibund community, and until this day we have not heard one word from anybody to suggest that the Om Mandali had anything political behind it.

A further article on Saturday June 17 drew attention to the inherent ridiculousness of resorting to the Criminal Law Amendment Act, passed in 1908 purely to quash terrorist and revolutionary uprisings in Bengal, to suppress the Om Mandali when

a movement calculated to produce an awakening among the womenfolk of their [Bhaibund] community cannot be smothered in such ruthless fashion . . . No one can deny that whatever the activities of the Mandali, it is they who were the victims of the lawless methods employed by Mukhi Mangharam and his friends, and that the Mandali sought its redress against them by entirely peaceful and constitutional methods. It is an incontrovertible fact, admitted in law courts, that the Mandali was obliged to leave Hyderabad on account of reasons of safety to protect itself against the unscrupulous methods employed by the Anti Om Mandali party.

The paper goes on to analyze what is meant by an "unlawful association" and argues that the activities of the Mandali could not possibly come under this definition.

But although the Anti party persisted in trying to get the Om Mandali shut down, the government took no further action—maybe because of the media reports—and the institution carried on as before. Members of the Anti party now took the view that, before long, Baba's money would run out, and the institution would disband of its own accord. But then they felt they could not wait for this eventuality, and they decided on one last desperate measure against the institution, and that was to send a hired assassin to kill Baba.

Some members of the Anti party found a Sikh bandit who seemed just the right person for the job: fierce, amoral, ruthless, used to killing, an out-and-out villain by all accounts. He was willing to do the deed for an appropriate sum of money, and a day was appointed when the bandit would break in, kill Baba with his curved sword and then be paid the blood money. Although the Om Mandali was by this time closely guarded, and Baba never allowed to be alone, security was unaccountably lax on this particular day, and the bandit managed to enter the building and gain access to Baba's room without much trouble.

When Baba looked round from his devotions and saw the bandit brandishing his sword, he knew immediately what he had come for. Yet perhaps neither bargained for what happened next. When he was no more than five feet away from Baba, the bandit suddenly became aware of a blinding, unearthly light, and was bathed in bliss in Baba's presence. The sword dropped from his hand and he could not carry out the deed. Then a sister came into the room with Baba's dinner, and saw the bandit herself. Terrified, she sounded the alarm, but Baba insisted that the bandit be fed before being allowed to leave. The bandit swore to observe nonviolence in the future and went home.

After this, the Anti party made no further attempts to discredit or demolish the Om Mandali, taking the view, perhaps, that it would soon die out of its own accord. And from then on, the founding group of between 250 and 300 people, of whom between fifty and sixty were men, were allowed to carry on their work without further interruption from ill-wishers, the state or the law.

Dada Vishwa Rattan, for many years in charge of finances at Mount Abu, was a college student of nineteen when the Om Mandali started hitting the headlines. He said:

I had read many accounts of the Om Mandali as they were all over Sind, and I became curious as to why the government was trying to ban the institution. Out of curiosity, I got permission to visit the Om Mandali in Karachi and found to my surprise that it was open to everybody, not a closed institution as I had thought. In those days, you had to write for permission to visit, and you would get a postcard back saying the time you could come. There were so many bungalows: It was a very big compound with many families living there. The sisters were giving classes, and immediately I was impressed with the quality of the information being imparted. After one week, I got permission to attend regular classes and I started wondering why there was such opposition. There would be at least a hundred pickets outside the building day and night. You would have to tread on them to get in, but I found a side entrance that was unguarded. It seemed to me that the sisters were very pure, and in fact

*radiated purity. I could not interest my parents in the insti-
tution, and when I told them I had become a child of God
they were very disappointed, as they wanted me to have a
good career and marriage, like everybody else. But nobody
and nothing could keep me away.*

*When I entered the institution, I became completely obe-
dient, doing everything I was asked. Although I had a science
degree, I used to stoke up the boiler for hot water, do shopping, cooking, washing, anything. I had been at the institution for a whole year before I even met Baba personally.*

The name of the institution now changed from Om
Mandali to Brahma Kumaris, and the time they spent
together in Karachi was known as the *yagya*, or sacrificial fire.
The idea was that the sisters (and brothers) should prepare
themselves for the work that lay ahead, namely, to take God's
new message to the whole world, and not just India.

In the meantime, the large group spent many hours in
meditation, contemplation and "churning"—a literal translation of the Hindi word for reflection. Every day Baba would
receive a new discourse while in a trance state, and this would
be transmitted to the group. Brahma Baba and the rest of the
group were all certain that the subject of the daily discourse
came directly from God.

The lives they led during these years were strictly disciplined, clean, pure and dedicated. The group members were
learning to regard themselves as souls rather than bodies, and
to separate themselves from all lust, desire and impurity.
They were becoming instruments for God's work.

Thus the early days of the Brahma Kumaris Institution

echoed the founding of several other religions, such as Judaism, Christianity and Islam, where prophets heard and foretold a new godly, sinless way of life—and later preached it to their community, usually amid much scorn, disbelief and persecution.

The big difference between the Brahma Kumaris and other spiritual movements, both ancient and modern, was that it was women, and very young women at that, who were being prepared to take the message into the world. In all major religions and spiritual movements of the past it has been men, and men only, who have been called. Although many early Christian martyrs and saints were women, they were not allowed or called on to be public preachers. The priestly caste, at least in codified religions, has always been male. Although Brahma Baba was the undoubted founder, the Brahma Kumaris from its earliest days put women (or souls in female bodies, in BK terminology) above men, as the only major spiritual movement ever to do so. The spiritual reasons for this will become apparent as the story progresses.

Before long, Om Radhe became known as "Mama" and ran the institution. Members many years older than her, both male and female, took notice of what she said, and gave her equal billing with Brahma Baba. She became seen as Saraswati, the Goddess of Wisdom in the Hindu pantheon.

Meanwhile, as the institution refined its teachings, doctrines and way of life, momentous events were happening in the outside world. There was the Second World War, and two years after that ended India won independence—and was divided into two. During these years the Om Mandali was largely left alone, as the media now had other things on its mind.

After Partition, in 1947, the province of Sind was incorporated into the new, mainly Muslim, country of Pakistan. Now, many members of the Hindu Bhaibund community fled Sind, fearing the worst, and established themselves in many parts of the world, rather like a Jewish diaspora. They went wherever they felt they could profitably trade, not just to India, and some started making huge fortunes anew.

The Brahma Kumaris Institution was never troubled by the Muslims. In fact, during the days of its persecution, it had been vigorously supported by many Muslim members of parliament. After Partition, leading Muslims, feeling that the BKs were a power for good, urged them to remain in Karachi.

But Brahma Baba, Mama and the others were increasingly feeling that they now belonged in India rather than in Pakistan. So they decided to move. But where should they go? How was the institution to be established elsewhere?

TWO

TO MOUNT ABU

The place decided on, after much deliberation, was Mount Abu, in Rajasthan.

Mount Abu has from earliest times been regarded as a holy place, with many religions and spiritual movements finding a home there. It had long been a place of pilgrimages for sages and saints, and the amazing Jain Dilwara temple, made of intricately carved marble and perfectly preserved since the eleventh century, is also there. In parts very beautiful, the area consists of a number of tribal villages, some extremely remote; farming land, forests, lakes and rocky climbs. It was a hill station in the British time, and very many boarding schools, hotels and government institutions established themselves there.

As the group arrived at the port of Karachi, many Pakistanis thronged the dock to say farewell, and were sad to see them go.

Some months previously one brother, Vishwa Kishore, had found a suitable house and grounds on Mount Abu, and this was purchased with Brahma Baba's permission. Jagdish Chander states in *Adi Dev* that the main reason for choosing Mount Abu was that it was in this place that the first deity, Brahma, had done his penance with the first goddess, Saraswati, 5,000 years previously; and all members of Om Mandali, now known as the *yagya*, now firmly believed that Baba and Mama were the reincarnation of those original deities. Therefore it was time to make Mount Abu once again a place of holiness and purity.

The house where they settled was renamed *Madhuban* — forest of honey — and their spiritual work and development continued. When not meditating and receiving discourses — called *murlis*, or the song of the flute, after the instrument played by Krishna in popular depictions — Brahma Baba was an indefatigable letter-writer. He wrote to most leading figures of the day, explaining the belief system of the Brahma Kumaris and the necessity of becoming soul-conscious rather than body-conscious.

One such letter was written to "Dear Soul in the form of King George," but it was unlikely that the shy, stammering and reluctant king, no great intellectual himself, could make much head or tail of the letter.

It read:

This world is an endless drama which repeats every 5,000 years. You are an actor in this great drama. Do you know that 5,000 years ago you acted in the same role as the King of England, in that same body at the same time and with the same name? And you will act the same role again after 5,000 years?

After expounding on this theme, the letter ended by saying: "We are sending you some literature in which these secrets are clearly explained."

Apart from anything else, King George VI was head of the Church of England, and this letter was written long before multiculturalism, or any such concept, was envisaged in the UK. Even though King George was technically *Ind. Imp.* or Emperor of India, before independence, there is no evidence that he studied, or was interested in, comparative religion — unlike his grandson Prince Charles.

To the Minister of State for Guwalior, Rahi Rajawade (a woman), Baba wrote:

Dear Friend,

The husband is considered guru and God for the wife. But only one who is passionless and completely pure can be called a God. Are the men of today passionless? Are they pure? The guru is said to make one realise the self and the Supreme; but the men of today are trapped in the pride of the body. So it is clear that men today are not worth being called either guru or God.

One can see from this letter that, far from being a traditional Hindu father and husband, Brahma Baba had now become a radical feminist, giving voice to sentiments that

might even seem extreme in the American feminist movement of the 1980s, let alone the hidebound India of the
1940s, when men were placed so far above women.

Hundreds, if not thousands, of these letters were sent to
leading dignitaries, heads of state, members of royal families
and religious leaders. Most of them, though, however carefully written and presented, fell on deaf ears and, as Jagdish
writes, "all this effort may have seemed without result, but it
was not so."

These letters gave members of the Brahma Kumaris practice, not only in setting out their ideas on paper, but in contacting and addressing leading world figures. Even if the
letters were unacknowledged and, perhaps, unread, they were
forays into the outside world, and, so far, the first forays made
to anybody outside their own community.

For fourteen years, ever since the Om Mandali began life
in Hyderabad, the Brahma Kumaris had been refining and
purifying themselves and their belief system in readiness for
the day when they would take their message into the world.
The many letters that were sent acted as a kind of advance
warning of their intention to spread the word so that everybody would eventually be able to hear and benefit from the
message.

Because of the way the caste system is constituted, traditional Hinduism cannot be a proselytizing religion, and so
few, if any, attempts have ever been made to convert those of
other beliefs. The first major evangelical faith was
Christianity, where disciples were ordered to go and spread the
gospel, which they duly did, so that eventually Christianity
became probably the most influential religion in the world.

The Brahma Kumaris were never intent on converting people to their particular way of thinking but were anxious to share some of the wisdom gained during those years of deep contemplation and study, to enable others to live more fulfilling, purposeful and, above all, peaceful, lives. They were seeing at firsthand the dramatic transformation brought about in the lives of those who became members of the Om Mandali, and could not help but be certain that the hand of God was at work.

One criticism often leveled at the BKs is that they have, from their earliest outreach times, targeted the famous and influential rather than the poor and needy. Almost all their early letters were sent to those at the very top of their particular tree. Nonentities were not initially contacted. The traditional BK response to this has been that if you target the influential you are more likely in that way to reach others down the line. And as their manpower (or rather, womanpower) resources were so limited in the early days, they had to pick and choose. There was also the factor that people tend naturally to address those most like themselves.

The Bhaibund community had long been used to dealing with powerful and influential people. Solidly middle class and rich itself, it naturally tended to gravitate to those broadly similar. Now invitations started coming from outside for members to go and spread the word, as it were.

But there was another, practical problem presenting itself at this time, and that was lack of money. The huge expense entailed in transporting several hundred people to Mount Abu had finally used up the last of Brahma Baba's once large fortune and so eventually the day the Anti party had long awaited had arrived, the day when there was simply nothing left in the kitty. Vishwa Rattan relates that one day they were literally down to their last quarter of a rupee.

He said: "Baba came to me one day and asked how much money I had in my pocket. I fished around and found this tiny coin. Baba said: 'That's all the money we have, then.' Most of the people in the *yagya* had come from very wealthy families, so it was a new challenge to all of us to be without money." At this point, Dada Vishwa Rattan added, many people, fearing for their future, left and rejoined their families, who were now mostly living in Bombay or Delhi, and who eagerly welcomed them back, free at last from the eccentric clutches of this most peculiar man.

But a core group remained, and as often seems to happen when there is unshakeable faith, well-wishers now started to send money, goods and services to enable the institution to continue. Rationing also prevailed at this time in India, and many essential goods, such as rice and wheat, were difficult to obtain even if you had the money. But somehow, goods and money came—sometimes at the eleventh and three-quarter hour. Also, by this time the mainly female members, who had been brought up to do nothing more strenuous than order meals from the household chef and dress themselves in rich clothes, had undergone many challenges. They had already defied their parents and husbands, they had refused sex, they had endured physical abuse and ill treatment, they had learned to cook and eat simple, inexpensive food.

Baba took the invitations coming from outside as a sign that it was now time to expand the institution's activities, to become outward-looking and to set up centers throughout

India. It had been decreed that sisters should be in charge of centers, that sisters should be the ones to spread the word, and so he now began suggesting this to those who were left. They knew the day had come but even so, they were initially terrified at the prospect when it became ever clearer that soon they would have to leave their cozy life with Baba and go forth into new, unknown and possibly hostile territory.

During the fourteen years of the *yagya*, when the Brahma Kumaris ran much like an enclosed order, the young girls and teenagers had grown up into women. Rama, later Dadi Prakashmani, was now twenty-nine and Om Radhe, or Mama, was thirty-two. No longer children, these were women who nevertheless had been brought up never to travel on their own, never to talk to a man other than a member of the family, never to be the first to say anything, but to wear a veil, keep their eyes downcast and do their best to pretend not to be there at all. And now, after having known nothing but seclusion, they were being asked to go out into India (and even elsewhere!) and tell others about their revelations and beliefs, beliefs that they knew would seem strange and unacceptable to their hearers. None were trained for any profession, none had public speaking skills, administration skills, writing skills. Many were also still very young.

One sister recalls: "I said to Baba, 'How can I go? I am just a little woman.' Baba replied: 'You are not a woman, Sister, you are a lioness.' So I went. But I was still terrified."

In spite of their terrors, they went forth, at first on the invitation of relatives and friends who would pay their train fares and put them up in houses, and later, as they gained confidence, under their own steam. In this way, small centers were started in Delhi, Lucknow, Calcutta, Bombay, Amritsar and Bangalore, each under the supervision of a sister.

Dadi Gulzar recalls the nightmare of trying to set up a center in Lucknow in the early 1950s:

> *I was in my early twenties, and had never traveled by myself before. In those days it was very unusual for women, particularly young women, to travel alone. As I got off the train I asked somebody: "Where do people stay in Lucknow?" I was directed to the nearest guest house and booked in, but it was horrible and I hated it. After a few days a Sindi family I knew came to visit and they were horrified at the dirty conditions I was living in. They took me to another guest house, and gradually two or three families started coming for classes.*
>
> *But I still had to find a permanent center. One person attending the classes said, "There are many vacant houses belonging to the government in Lucknow: You must get hold of one of those." "But how?" I asked. I was told I had to write a letter to the chief minister, but I was worried that he would either not get it or, if he got it, wouldn't bother to read it from a nobody like me. Eventually I learned that the chief minister would be at a public meeting, so I went along, determined to meet him in person. By this time two other sisters had joined me. The minister was a very elderly man, very important, and everybody else gasped when we went to speak to him. He asked why we were here and I replied that we were giving God's message and needed somewhere to live. "You are the chief minister," I reminded him, "and the only one who can help us. I have a letter here for you to sign and I will not move until you sign it."*

He said, "Give me the letter," and immediately wrote on it, giving permission for us to stay in a government house for three months. When that time was up, we got another three months after seeing the minister again. After that we got a place of our own, donated by a wealthy person.

When asked what gave her the courage to go up and speak to the minister, Dadi replied: "All my courage and enthusiasm came from God. That was what gave me the power to do things I would never have dared do on my own. I was completely naïve, and had been in the Om Mandali since the age of eight, but still, I did it."

In 1954, greatly daring, Dadi Prakashmani, later the administrative head, went with a delegation to the World Religious Congress in Japan. On their return, the party also visited Hong Kong, Malaysia, Indonesia and Singapore, although at that time no permanent centers were set up. Nowadays, all these places have thriving centers.

As with the early Christians, these pioneer women did not have an easy ride. Indians were not used to hearing women preach or give spiritual classes or, for that matter, doing anything on their own initiative, and they were shocked and outraged. Dr. Johnson's notorious sexist remark about women preachers is too well-known to repeat, but in India the situation was twenty thousand times worse, as women were not even officially allowed to preach the scriptures at all.

But what was worse was that they were preaching their own material, a new religion as it seemed, and one that went against orthodox beliefs in many significant aspects. Men who paid these physically small, white-clad and meek-seeming sisters any attention risked rough treatment themselves from mobs who stormed the newly established centers.

Jagdish, who became a dedicated BK in 1953, recalls those times:

> One particular religious sect organized a gathering to protest at the Brahma Kumaris. They were throwing stones at the centers and publishing criticisms in the local papers. Once they knew I was involved, a mob got hold of me and started beating me up. I was very badly hurt, but had already learned from Baba that we should not be angry, that such people are our brothers and they are acting in ignorance. But feelings against the BKs were so intense that people followed us, called us names and set out to close the centers. In one place, a whole town was against us, and religious and political leaders joined forces to get us shut down. At the time, we had very little money, no public influence and no prominent people on our side.

Why was there such opposition once more? Jagdish explains:

> The sisters were giving teachings that people did not understand. They thought they were Christians in disguise, as Christians have always been known to preach the gospel, and that they were trying to convert everybody. It was also given out that the BKs were against the scriptures; our Hindu scriptures, that is. The other continuing problem was celibacy, and there were very many court cases in the 1950s where a husband tried to force his wife back to him for sexual purposes.

Jagdish added: "Women in those days had no social status, no voice, no freedom and yet here they were, daring to preach as though they were gurus or sadhus."

Jagdish, who at the time was a young man in his early twenties, was attracted to the BKs because he could not deny what he experienced in meditation and yoga in their presence:

I would get detached, and feel I was in a sea of light. It was such a peaceful experience, and as if I was completely cut off from my surroundings. These would appear vague and luminous, unreal. I had no control over these experiences. When I met Brahma Baba in Madhuban, I was transported into another realm altogether, within minutes. All others sitting there disappeared from sight. I had lost all sense of space and time. I had long wanted to have a direct experience of God and now I was certain I was having such an experience. But I also felt that the information, the knowledge the BKs were sharing, was the truth.

At the time in charge of a teacher training college near Delhi, Jagdish had from his earliest youth studied the scriptures of many religions: Hindu, Buddhist, Muslim, Christian. But he was instantly convinced on hearing the BKs that their interpretation of world events was far more rational and logical than any previous explanation.

"I still had many questions," he said. "But for the moment I put them aside, as I could not deny the experience. And I reasoned that it was possible that what I had read in other scriptures was either wrong, or a misinterpretation."

It might be a good idea at this point to outline briefly the belief system of the Brahma Kumaris, as it had been revealed to the group at this time. The overwhelming understanding was that we are all primarily souls, rather than bodies, and that it is the soul that drives the body and brain. The soul is the driver, with the body being the car and its engine. Once we can see ourselves as souls inhabiting bodies rather than the other way round, the BK taught, there can be no such thing as racism, sexism, casteism.

The soul itself is seen as being an eternal, nonphysical, nondimensional entity possessing three main characteristics. These are mind, intellect and behavioral tendencies, known in Hindi as *sanskars*. Because the soul is eternal, it will go through many different births, and each successive birth is determined by the law of karma, or action. This law states that whatever actions we perform, for good or ill, will return to us in like form—eventually. As we sow, so shall we reap, although the harvest may come about in another body than the present one.

An analogy often used by the BKs to bring home the doctrine of the eternal soul is that of actors on a stage. An actor in one play may have just a walk-on part; in another be the central character. But whatever the parts, they are not "him." As soon as he removes the costume, he stops playing that particular part. So it is with successive incarnations. In one birth we may be of high degree; in another a pauper or outcast. It is all an eternal drama, with us all playing a part, and our bodies are simply temporary costumes which are eventually cast aside. And with every successive birth the soul develops more layers, or *sanskars*, as impressions of each incarnation, for good or ill, remain. There is no such thing, they teach, as an action without due consequences, either to ourselves or others.

God, according to BK doctrine, is seen as eternal, non-physical, nonmaterial and as One, as the Supreme Soul. There is only one God and he is the same person, or the same concept, as Jahweh, Jehovah, Shiva, Allah in other religions. Although God is seen in most religions and spiritual traditions as "he," in fact the ever-incorporeal being is neither male nor female, as he does not possess a body or physical form. He does not ever descend into matter, although from time to time he may "borrow" a body to speak through at critical times in human history. Thus, he spoke through the early prophets, through Jesus Christ, through Mohammed, through Brahma Baba. But these beings, although perhaps divine instruments, are not God. They remain human and, as such, should not be worshipped although they can be admired and respected.

Traditional Hinduism is full of ritual, and BKs do not believe in ritual. God should be remembered, and all we do should be in remembrance of him, but that does not mean we should bow down or abase ourselves to any image or representation of God.

At such times as God "borrows" a human body, fundamental truths are revealed, or re-revealed. Then that person becomes God's messenger. The reason why some people rather than others are chosen is an eternal mystery. BKs are often asked: Why Brahma Baba? Why choose a self-made millionaire, a family man already elderly, rather than a young, unencumbered seeker after truth? Wasn't it odd of God to choose Brahma Baba?

But then, if you think about it, they say, Jesus Christ was an odd choice as well. Why did God not pick an influential

Roman or prominent Jew instead of a carpenter's son, a nobody? Most of God's chosen have been oddballs, in one way or another, people who have not easily fitted into the life around them. And all have displayed immense courage, for most have been preaching a message that went against current orthodoxy, and have therefore been regarded as dangerous subversives.

The reason why Brahma Baba was chosen could not easily be answered in the 1950s, although the answer has become clearer with time and will, I hope, emerge satisfactorily in later chapters.

BKs also teach, in common with other Eastern religions, that time is cyclical, not linear. As such, it endlessly repeats. Time has no beginning and no end, but each cycle goes through several stages. First of all there is the Golden Age, where everything is perfect and there is eternal spring. This time is remembered in the Bible as the Garden of Eden and in the Koran as the Garden of Allah. After this comes the Silver Age, when things become slightly more degenerate. This is followed by the more decadent Copper Age, and finally we have the Iron Age, our own present age, characterized by greed, lust, attachment, violence, fraud, racism, sexism and every kind of vice. The concept of these Four Ages is also found in traditional Hindu scriptures, and is the complete antithesis of evolution theories, which hold that we are constantly progressing, evolving and improving. Eastern scriptures maintain that as souls interact ever more with matter through the ages there is degeneration rather than improvement.

Towards the end of the Iron Age, BKs believe, God reveals

himself (through Brahma Baba) and this momentous event heralds an Age of Transition where all bad is wiped out (we'll see how later) and a new Golden Age begins again.

The BKs believe that each cycle of time lasts for 5,000 years, with each age spanning 1,250 years—exactly. Then it repeats itself identically. As Baba wrote to King George, you will play this same part again, in every detail, that you are playing now—in another 5,000 years.

This interpretation of how time continues has occasioned worldwide astonished debate, as neither Easterners nor Westerners find it easy to comprehend or accept. At this stage, we will just say that whatever length of time evolutionists and others have put upon planet Earth, there are no written records going back more than about 3,000 years, and that is a fact. Are we, BKs ask, to believe that humans existed for millions of years before they learned to read and write? Also, there has never in recorded time been any evidence of one species changing into another. Nor have any scientists ever observed such a phenomenon.

At least, protagonists for this theory maintain, the BK interpretation has exact numbers, and a kind of logic and rationality behind it. And the BKs go further in their exactitude. The maximum number of births, they say, for a human soul during each cycle or *kalpa* is eighty-four, although not all souls will take so many births. All the time during each 5,000 year cycle new souls are coming down to Earth, which explains the ever-increasing population, and the idea of "new" souls and "old" souls.

This insistence on exact numbers may be one reason why

so many BKs, at least in India, are qualified mathematicians and accountants!

As to the doctrine of transmigration of souls, held by many Hindu-based movements, no species, BKs maintain, can ever transmute into another. Human souls cannot descend into animal bodies, and animal souls cannot take birth in the body of a human. Although BKs believe that animals have souls, these stay all the time in the same species of animal. When asked whether bacteria or viruses have souls, they laugh and admit that God has not vouchsafed this information. But, at that level, does it matter? They also do not imagine that there can be life on other planets, and tell people that, in their opinion, there are no such things as aliens, UFOs or other extraterrestrial entities.

Without going into the depths of comparative religion at this stage, we have to be aware that on two very important points these beliefs differ from traditional Hinduism enough to make traditional Hindus very angry. One is monism: Hindus believe that matter, soul and God are different manifestations of the same thing, and that God is everywhere, or omnipresent. (Although this argument may seem academic to many Westerners, it has caused much schism between BKs and orthodox Hindus in India.) The other main aspect of Hinduism is the importance given to ritual, ceremonial and devotional, all of which are dispensed with by BKs. The meditation is open-eyed and nowadays there is no chanting, although quiet music is played to encourage and enhance a meditative state.

"There was also the aspect," said Jagdish, "that the BKs

were maintaining that our great Indian sages were wrong. 'How could they be wrong?' people asked."

The BK lifestyle disciplines developed during the years of seclusion also did not endear them to the traditionalists. For one thing, they would not eat (and still won't, come to that) food prepared by non-BKs, and this offends ingrained notions of hospitality. They did not marry, they did not have families and they were preaching heretical doctrines. They were against physical sex, not just for dedicated members, but for everybody wishing to follow a spiritual way of life. Nor did they ever ask for any money for their classes or courses, unlike many gurus, and that was weird in itself. However did they support themselves? No wonder they seemed strange, otherworldly and unreal.

But, as ever, when people seem to be speaking sincerely from the heart, when they have the strength and faith to practice as they preach, to "walk their talk," some key people will pick up, hear and understand the message. And once they have the conviction that they have heard the truth, nothing on Earth will prevent these people from following this path, however unusual or unacceptable it may seem to the majority.

This is how it was for Jagdish, who soon could not be persuaded to lead any other life. Two other men who heard the early call were Nirwair Singh and Ramesh Shah, men who have since played a major part in the efficient running and growth of the organization.

Ramesh first came across the BKs in 1953, when a youth of nineteen studying law and accountancy in Bombay.

In 1950, when I was sixteen, my father died of heart failure, and my mother was broken-hearted. She became permanently depressed, and nothing I or my two sisters could do made any difference. I tried to take her to gurus, but nothing helped. In 1953 a small BK center opened in Bombay, and my mother started going. From then, there was a dramatic change in her behavior and attitude. What we had not managed for three years, the BKs managed in fifteen days. She found the yoga teaching so uplifting and inspiring she asked me to go to a meeting, to try it for myself. For her sake, I went.

At the meeting, the sister in charge went into trance (this does not happen nowadays) and gave a trance message from my father, saying he was in the habit of chewing betel nut and paan, which was true. When I got home, I asked my mother why she was telling the sisters about father's bad habits. She said: "But I never said anything." One Sunday my mother invited some sisters to our house, and I thought I would test them out, so I asked the one who had been in trance to pick out my father's photo. As a keen photographer I had around 3,000 pictures, but she picked out my father instantly. She had seen him in trance.

I thought then that these sisters must have some spiritual power, but at the time I could not accept Brahma Baba, and I became a student of the Bhagavad Gita.

In 1960 Ramesh married Usha, after an exotic encounter:

I was doing Patanjali yoga, very popular at the time, and around 4,000 students were attending. Usha, another student who I had not met at the time, kept seeing a clear picture of a human being, rather than Krishna, while meditating, although she did not know who this person was. When she asked her guru about it, saying that the image of this person was disturbing her greatly, the guru said: "This is the person you are destined to marry, and I will introduce you." The guru knew that person was me, and introduced me to Usha, who gasped in astonishment, as she recognized the person she had seen in yoga. After we got to know each other a little, and our families had been introduced, Usha asked if I would be prepared to have a celibate marriage.

I said: "I will do my level best," and we married in 1960. In 1961 we both joined the BKs after going to Madhuban, and dedicated ourselves completely.

Although I initially found the concept of Brahma Baba difficult, everything changed when Usha and I went to Madhuban. Baba was giving a class on the difference between love and attachment, and as I listened, I knew he understood that difference. Then the bliss and happiness I experienced in yoga was different from anything I had known before. I feel now that this knowledge gives an inner development and inner strength greater than that found in any other spiritual path.

Has Ramesh kept his long-ago vow of celibacy? His reply: "One hundred percent. Ours has always been a spiritual, not a physical, marriage." He and Usha have never had children, and have both worked tirelessly on behalf of the BKs ever since the early 1960s, although Ramesh has also continued to run his accounting business. His mother is still alive, at the time of this writing in her nineties, and his elder sister is also a dedicated BK. "And Mother never became depressed again since meeting the BKs," Ramesh attests.

When asked how he has coped with women being in charge, Ramesh says: "I think of the older women as mothers, of my contemporaries as sisters, and of the younger women as daughters. Then there is no problem."

Nirwair Singh, whom we met briefly in the Prologue, has lived at Mount Abu as a completely dedicated BK since the early 1960s. As his name suggests, he came from a Sikh background, and after college joined the Indian navy with the intention of becoming a career officer.

However, once he came into contact with the BK sisters, he knew that these would be the waters he henceforth charted, rather than those designated for him by the Indian navy.

Here is his story:

I was always interested in electronics, and had completed all my courses by 1958. A year later, I came into contact with the BKs in Bombay through a friend. We later went to a center in Delhi run by Jagdish and Dadi Gulzar (the one who had experienced startling visions at the age of eight, and who was now in her late twenties). I had always been interested in meditation and spiritual pursuits, but there was something about the atmosphere at the centers that intrigued me. We were given the seven-day course by a sister of about sixteen, and at the time we had turbans and long beards. At first the young sister was nervous about letting us in, as she wanted to check we were genuine, and not out to attack the center.

From the first, I was fascinated by the exactness of the knowledge. As an electronics engineer, the logic appealed to me. But that alone wouldn't have made me give up my career to dedicate myself to the Brahma Kumaris. What happened was that on the fourth day of the course, when we meditated, I had a powerful experience of self-realization. The sister looked just like an angel, and the whole room was filled with a subtle pink light which dazzled me. I felt then that I was not in my body, but was a being of light. It was a transcendental experience and so wonderful I had to try and repeat it. Eight friends of mine from the navy joined one by one, and gradually we also became vegetarian.

When I rejoined my ship, a destroyer, I had a new concept of myself being peaceful, loveful and above petty squabbles. But one particular incident made me think again about my chosen profession. In 1960 the Indian government tried to drive out the Portuguese from Indian territories. We were assigned to take over the island of Anjadiv after being given the intelligence that it was uninhabited.

At the time I was a junior commissioned officer, looking after radar and underwater detection sets. When our people landed on the island, immediately the Portuguese opened fire and shot eight men dead, injuring another eight. Our intelligence, therefore, had been wrong.

Instantly the Indians retaliated by opening fire, and themselves killed eight men. At this the Portuguese raised the white flag. There were no civilians on this island as it happened, but for a little piece of land we had killed nearly twenty people. After that event, I started thinking about serving humanity rather than killing them.

The essence of raja yoga, as taught by the BKs, was that you could attain 100 percent peace, purity, happiness and serenity. Mama [Om Radhe], who was aged thirty-nine then, came to Bombay and was considered by the group to be the goddess of knowledge. She was a singer and dancer before becoming a BK, and the first administrative head of the organization. Even her own mother called her Mama, and I had a blissful transcendental experience in her presence.

The upshot was that on November 20, 1963, my twenty-fifth birthday, I left the navy and came to Mount Abu as a full-time BK. There were at the time just nine people living full time in Madhuban; there were twenty-five centers and around 5,000 surrendered people, all Indians.

Nirmala Kajaria qualified as a medical doctor in Bombay in the 1950s, and she came into contact with the BKs in 1961.

I had not grown up with the organization, but I always had two aims in life. One was to remain pure, or celibate, and the other was to be independent. Both were very unusual aims for girls in the 1950s, as was the ambition to study and become a doctor, but my father was happy to go along with my wishes, and allowed me to attend medical school. My ultimate aim at the time was to practice medicine in villages, to be a kind of barefoot doctor.

I never wanted to be wealthy or famous, but to be able to help people with my medical studies. So when I came into contact with the BKs it was easy for me to have the resolve to remain single. I felt straight away that this path was right for me, and would allow me to focus on what I wanted.

For the first three years of her BK life, Nirmala lived with her family, then, with money she had saved up from her work as a doctor, bought a house for the BKs in Bombay, so that a proper center could be established there.

"With the BKs I found peace, stability and happiness. I am certain that I could not have experienced these qualities as a traditional Hindu, especially as in the 1950s families had to come first with women."

So, gradually, people of quality and dedication were being attracted. All, however intellectual or rational by character or education, say that much as they might like and appreciate the knowledge and information, what made them dedicate was the "supersensuous bliss" experienced in meditation. In other words, it was the *feelings* they experienced, the way that the yoga practice touched their heart, that made the possibility of any other kind of life fade away, rather than the appeal to their minds or intellect.

The Brahma Kumaris World Spiritual University, as it was now called, was establishing itself in many parts of India, although during the 1960s protests and marches against it continued. It also had mainly adverse press coverage. But every year the opposition grew more feeble, as the BKs gained in confidence and as their numbers increased, especially among professionals.

But during the later part of the 1960s two events were to test their strength and resolve to the utmost. One was the sudden, unexpected death of Mama in 1965, aged forty-five, from breast cancer, and the other was the death of Brahma Baba on January 18, 1969. Aged ninety-three, he died suddenly from a mild heart attack just after the evening discourse ended at around nine o'clock.

Although Baba's death was not entirely unexpected on account of his age, Mama was in her prime when she died. Also, she had been joint administrative head for very many years, and her death dealt the still-struggling organization a very severe setback, almost a body blow. However would they manage without Mama?

But they did. Sister Manmohini, affectionately known as Didi, took the place of Mama as additional administrative head and, after the death of Baba in 1969, Sister Prakashmani was appointed administrative head of the entire organization. The trust originally established by Brahma Baba, consisting of nine women, continued, and plans were soon set in motion to undertake the biggest challenge yet: that of taking Baba's message outside India—and to the West.

THREE

LONDON

Anybody in the West who has had even a peripheral connection with the Brahma Kumaris will have come into contact
with, or at least heard of, Dadi Janki, the additional administrative head of the university, who has been in charge of over-
seas service since 1974. One of the physically tiniest of the
BKs, Dadi is considerably less than five feet in height, looks
rather like Yoda in the film *Star Wars*, and still, after more
than a quarter of a century in the West, speaks only in her
native Hindi.

Physically unimposing, rather shy in company and almost
totally lacking in small talk, Dadi Janki has nevertheless been
almost single-handedly responsible for the dramatic and far-
reaching impact the Brahma Kumaris have made in the West.
A tireless traveler, she constantly jets from one continent and

country to another, holding meetings, giving talks, hosting programs and supervising plans for expansion in all parts of the world.

Her presence is always peaceful, always benign, and full of power and love. Few people have ever seen Dadi Janki in a bad mood, cross or expressing frustration. Over the years, she has good-humoredly subjected herself to a number of scientific experiments, some of which have shown her, according to U.S. scientists, to have "the most stable mind we have ever tested." She has appeared at the Albert Hall with psychic Uri Geller, given talks and presentations at the House of Lords in London, at the United Nations Headquarters in New York, at major peace conferences and gatherings all over the world, and been a speaker at gatherings of eminent scientists, doctors, lawyers, politicians, environmentalists and feminist groups.

It seems that no group is too large or too small, too important or too unimportant, for Dadi to address. She is as at home addressing a summit conference of world leaders as speaking to a small group about whether to redecorate the outside of a building. She gives the same dedicated attention to all projects she involves herself in, and is in constant demand for lifestyle advice from the many people she sees on an individual basis.

She also keeps herself up-to-date, making full use of e-mail, the Internet, mobile phones, satellite connections, headphones, videos and other electronic equipment.

When meeting people, Dadi genuinely sees not the clothes, the color, the race or rank, but the pure, peaceful soul beneath all the trappings. But to arrive at this benevolent vision of humanity, when so many people are full of all kinds of negativity, has taken many years of long, hard work on the self, and has required the development of an inner core of self-confidence and unshakeable inner peace, maintained and strengthened by daily meditation.

As Dadi Janki firmly rejects any special treatment for herself, and always wears a plain cotton sari (or, nowadays, more probably, polyester), she looks very ordinary, just another elderly Indian lady who you could easily overlook in a large gathering.

But she is not ordinary, and her story provides a vivid example of how absolute determination and single-mindedness can overcome all obstacles, even those seemingly impossible. The almost palpable aura of calmness and peace she now exudes has been forged in steel, as she has in her life faced challenges that would have daunted most women.

I like to think of Dadi Janki as a spiritual suffragette and in some ways the struggles she has endured, and the strength needed to face and overcome them, are reminiscent of the hunger strikes, prison sentences and other privations suffered by those women who fought for female enfranchisement in the UK during the early years of the twentieth century.

As we have seen, Hindu women in the Bhaibund community in the 1930s had no rights, no education, no choices in life and no status or power of their own at all. Dadi Janki came from this community and was, on the face of it, as powerless as all the others. The difference was that she did not accept her powerless state, and fought against it until she won the right to decide her own fate.

She was born in Sind in 1916, and her wealthy family was closely connected with that of Brahma Baba. Baba's uncle and Dadi's uncle, both jewelers, were very close friends, both known for their religious devotion and also their large contributions to charity. Dadi's father was also spiritually inclined, and Dadi's family all attended Brahma Baba's satsangs before any of them knew or understood what was happening.

All we knew at the time [Dadi said through her interpreter Manda] was that something very powerful was going on. I witnessed a lot of transformation in the people who attended. It was as if something magical was happening, and I could not keep away. I had the very strong feeling that I had found what I had been looking for, and did not need to look any further. I knew that I did not want marriage, a family and an ordinary life for myself. I had known this from my earliest years, even though there seemed no possibility of any other kind of existence.

At the time of those early gatherings, Dadi was aged nineteen and unmarried. Although her family was rich, it was considered a waste of money to educate daughters, and so Dadi Janki received just three years of formal education. She did not have enough education to follow a profession, or to secure financial independence for herself. It was taken for granted that she would marry as soon as she reached a certain age, and that a suitable husband would be found for her. This duly happened. A prospective husband was lined up, a wedding date set.

While the arrangements were being made, Dadi continued to assert that she would never marry. This happened right up to and including the very day of the wedding:

Brahma Baba had said to my father, don't make her get married if she doesn't want to, but in the end my father bowed to social custom. In our community at that time it would never do to have a nineteen-year-old daughter unmarried. On the morning of the wedding, I said to my father: "Send the bridegroom away, I don't want to get married. I'm not going downstairs. I'm not going through with it, cancel the wedding."

I was very insistent, but even so, the marriage went through. This was in 1937 when I was aged twenty. Afterwards, I had to go to live at my new husband's house, as was the custom. I was very upset about it all and said to the young man, "What you want I don't want, and what I want you don't want. We are not suited to each other in any way." But my husband wouldn't listen, and tried to bind me to him by any means possible.

He was supposed to be in business in Calcutta, but for the next fourteen months he never stirred out of the house, for fear that I would leave and go to Baba the minute his back was turned. Which of course I would have done. So he became my constant minder, never letting me out of his sight.

He also wanted me to dress extravagantly and parade me around, but I refused. He tried to make me go to the cinema and other social occasions with him, but again I refused. I said to him: "If I'm not allowed to go to religious activities, I am certainly not going to these others with you."

Nor was I allowed to read Baba's discourses, or murlis. But with another sister, Didi—the one who succeeded Mama as head of the organization—I devised a way to be able to read them anyway. Didi would send the murlis *down the drainpipes of the houses until they reached our house, when I would retrieve them and read them. In order to read them, I had to lock myself in the bathroom and read them secretly. It was much like being a prisoner of war, and all the time I was plotting my escape. I have never had physical love for anybody, and I did not want the bondage of being married, especially to a young man who was not interested in my concerns.*

My husband was keeping such a close eye on me that I daren't get directly in touch with the Om Mandali. He had forbidden me to make any contact. He also became violent and brutal. And all the time he was telling me not to go to the Mandali, not to speak to any members there, he kept hitting me on the head. He hit me so hard that I couldn't even comb my hair, my head was so painful. When he was hitting me, he was shouting: "Are you remembering Dada Lekhraj? Are you? Are you?" He wanted to knock it out of me, quite literally.

But there was worse to come. According to Baba's precepts, I was determined to remain celibate. I wanted to live a pure life and not to have sexual relations. But my husband would not condone this behavior and he forced himself on me. I was horribly shocked at this, and the consequence was that I had a child, a son. The first child is normally an occasion for rejoicing in an Indian household, especially if the child is a boy, but I only felt bondage. I had not chosen the marriage or the husband, and I had not chosen to bring a new life into the world. As it was, this boy only lived for four months and though his death was very sad, I see it now as a blessing in disguise. Baba was protecting me from earthly bondages.

I was not allowed to have visitors, just in case they found a way of smuggling me to Baba, so it was a very lonely, unhappy time. But I never gave up hope.

Dadi's behavior in her husband's house was not calculated to endear her to her in-laws. For one thing, she would go into the kitchen and cook her own food, refusing to eat what they ate. They were shocked by this as the household employed not only a chef but plenty of servants to do the cooking. The other thing that displeased them was that Dadi refused to sit around gossiping. She would say: "I'm not sitting around in idle chat." Instead, she would get out the Bhagavad Gita and while pretending to read it, start to meditate and remember Baba.

Dadi also found a way of being independent. She would do very fine embroidery and give it to her family as gifts to distribute to others so that in her mind she would not be in financial bondage to anybody. When asked why she spent so much time sewing, she would reply that this was her hobby, and she enjoyed doing it.

"Through these challenges," said Dadi, "my internal strength grew. I wanted to be able to say that nobody was feeding me or keeping me. It seemed that I had these tendencies towards independence from a very early age, and they were certainly not the standard tendencies of passive dependent Indian females of the time."

When Dadi's father saw how unhappy his daughter was in her marriage, he himself surrendered to Brahma Baba in Hyderabad and went with his family, consisting of four other daughters, to live with the Om Mandali. Meanwhile, Dadi was still stranded at her husband's home.

I felt that eventually Baba would call me and release me from bondage. One day one of my sisters came to visit me, but she was not allowed to see me on my own. My husband sat and watched us closely as we talked, to make sure I was not plotting anything he might not like. But that day I finally developed enough power to leave. I began to have a dangerously high fever which they thought was TB, and the doctor was instantly called. He said, "She is so ill because she is unhappy and the only way to make her better is to give her happiness." Then the doctor asked me what I wanted, and I told him I missed my mother and father and sisters, who were all by this time in Karachi with Dada Lekhraj, a journey of five or six hours by train.

Of course by this time the Om Mandali had suffered very bad publicity, court cases and persecution from the Anti party. My husband, who had been listening to the doctor said to me: "Okay, I'll take you to Karachi, let's go."

When we got there, I told my husband that I was very sick and not well enough to leave. But the next day he said: "We can go back now." He felt he had made enough of a concession. I told him that I would go with him on condition that he attended to his business in Calcutta and stopped watching me every minute of the day. I said I was not a caged bird, and I was also very ill.

He gave in and went to Calcutta, with very many misgivings. After arriving back in Hyderabad, I made my plans. I got out my jewelry box, separated my own jewelry from that given to me by my in-laws, and gave my own jewelry to my father, when he came to visit me from Karachi. I also told my father that I was leaving my husband to go to

Karachi permanently. The jewelry was to provide me with money for myself. I left the stuff given to me by my in-laws for them to find.

My father, seeing that I was absolutely adamant, now agreed to help me and he said he would come at night to enable me to escape. That night I put on a white sari and shawl, took a cab to the station with my father and we arrived in Karachi early next morning. Then I sent a telegram to my in-laws saying: "Consider me dead."

On receipt of the telegram, my husband came running to Karachi. But before he arrived, I went to see a lawyer about getting divorced, telling the lawyer my husband had caused me so much physical pain, and was brutal to me. I gave the lawyer a list of things he had done to me and requested police protection if he came after me.

When my husband arrived, with some of his family, at my father's house in the Om Mandali complex, he had a car waiting to take me back. He picked a time when my father wasn't there and the servants let him in. I was upstairs at the time, and as soon as my husband saw me, he picked me up in his arms and carried me downstairs. I was a very tiny skinny thing in those days and very light, like a child. I screamed and screamed and in the end, screamed so loud that he dropped me. Before he recovered his wits, I managed to rush upstairs and lock the door on him.

My husband didn't want to be caught behaving like this, especially as I had already complained about his treatment of me to the lawyer. So, in the end, he and his family all got into the car and left without retrieving me.

After that, his sister came to see me and said: "What do you think you are doing? You've lost him his honor and we'll have to get him married again." But there was no way I was ever going back to him, no matter what anybody said or did.

"Less than a week later," said Dadi, "he remarried, and finally, I was free." Dadi joined the Om Mandali permanently in 1939, in Karachi. In later years her former husband, named Naval, became very ashamed of his brutal behavior, and eventually came to worship Dadi, although he never surrendered or became a BK himself.

In the early 1950s, during the "beggary" period when all the money had run out and nobody knew where the next rupee was coming from, Dadi Janki often wondered what she was meant to be doing with her life. One day at Mount Abu she had a vision where Brahma Baba became like a globe of light carried around the whole world.

"After that," Dadi said, "I had the very strong feeling that the word must be spread round the world, not just in India, and that I would very probably be the one to take this message to other countries. Throughout the 1950s, though, while I was running centers and classes in India, there seemed no way of achieving this.

"Finally, in 1969, came the glimmer of a possibility."

That "glimmer" was provided by another remarkable woman, a teenager more than thirty years Dadi Janki's junior. This woman was Jayanti Kirpalani, a distant relative of Brahma Baba's, who was in the unique position of being Indian yet with an English background and education. Jayanti, born in India in 1949, had come with her parents to

London at the age of eight, and passed the eleven-plus to attend a London girls' grammar school, gaining many O and A levels. She was at the time the only Indian girl in the school.

At the time her serious BK involvement started, Jayanti was aged nineteen and rather reluctantly studying pharmacy at London University. Like Dadi Janki so many years earlier, Jayanti had made up her mind from an early age that she did not want to get married and have a family, even though a marriage had been arranged for her by her grandparents when she was just one year old.

Nor did Jayanti particularly want to be a pharmacist. She had originally meant to train as a doctor, but had failed to gain a place at any London teaching hospital. Although she had the paper qualifications to be accepted at a medical school, two things had stood in her way. One was that she was Indian; the other was that she was female and, at the time, only 20 percent of intake at medical schools could be female. This unfairness aroused the feminist in Jayanti, and she decided to dedicate herself to working for female equality in the world.

But her underlying reason for wanting to be a doctor was not so much a burning desire to administer medicine as to be financially independent, and a medical qualification seemed the best way of securing this. Jayanti reasoned that doctors have a lot of respect, earn good salaries and that also, if she became a doctor, the pressure on her to marry and have a family would be that much less because she would then have a respected vocation.

Becoming a pharmacist was very much second-best, especially as Jayanti's natural bent was not really towards science, but the arts. However, a pharmacy qualification would still enable her to earn her own living and remain independent. But after being at university for a few months, Jayanti started to become dissatisfied, and decided to take some time out to "find herself" and explore her native India.

Although not particularly religious as a teenager—she had wanted to be a modern sixties London girl like her class-mates—Jayanti had in fact grown up knowing all about the Brahma Kumaris, as her mother had herself become a BK in 1957. Jayanti said:

My mother became a fully dedicated BK in 1957, although she continued to live with her family rather than at a center, and she was actually one of Dadi Janki's early students. Soon after that my father decided to come to England to run his import/export business. My mother was devastated, and asked Baba in Delhi: "How am I going to survive if I go abroad? There are no centers, no other people in the world outside India following these disciplines and way of life."

Baba told her it would be okay and when we moved to London—my mother, father, younger brother and myself, aged eight—she continued to receive the murlis, *sent from India. She then started to hold little meetings in her home of other expatriate Indians who had known Baba and who were interested in the teachings.*

We still visited India fairly regularly, and I first met Baba when I was eight years old. Baba told me then that I would become a spiritual teacher but at that age I was hardly interested, and although Indian, I grew up very much as a

Western teenager. I used to read Barbara Cartland and Mills and Boon romances in bed at night, and loved them, even though I never envisaged such a life for myself.

But I did become very Western, especially as I was the only Indian girl in my school until I reached the sixth form. But in 1968 I took time off from university to go to Pune, where Dadi Janki was running a center at the time.

When I met Dadi, she was so powerful that something awoke a spark of spirituality in me. From that time on, I decided I wanted to dedicate my life to the Brahma Kumaris. As this organization was run and administered by women, the only one I knew of which was, either spiritual or secular, it seemed a good way of combining my feminist instincts with my spiritual yearnings. After I had been in India for some months studying the BK teachings, I told Brahma Baba that I wanted to dedicate my life to the BKs, and over the next few months I prepared myself to do service in India.

At the time, said Jayanti, there was no thought in her mind of coming back to the UK. In October 1968 Baba sent her to Agra, site of the Taj Mahal, for the purpose of serving foreigners who came as tourists to India. Jayanti decided then not to continue her university studies, and she remained in India. By this time she had abandoned her Western clothes and hairstyle and adopted the BK uniform of plain white sari and long pigtail down her back, making her look like a traditional Indian woman once more. She last met Baba in December 1968 in Mount Abu, just before he died, and remained in India until June 1969, when she decided to return to London.

There were two reasons to come back. One was to satisfy myself that this was the life I truly wanted, and, second, Dadi Janki had been saying to me for some time that a lot of people, not just Indians, wanted to experience peace. At the time, I thought that nobody in the West would possibly want to hear about Baba's teachings, or to experience peace. Unlike Dadi Janki, I had grown up in the West and knew at firsthand what it was like.

By mid-1969, the Brahma Kumaris World Spiritual University had been established in India for thirty-three years. But even though India was *par excellence* the land of gurus, saints and sages, the institution had never been given an easy ride. Although now tolerated by the authorities, BKs were still considered somewhat eccentric and subversive, and certainly not part of the spiritual mainstream. In fact, protests against the movement lasted in India right up until the mid-1980s.

Their teachings did not please the orthodox Hindus, largely because the BKs were teaching from their own texts received during trance states, the *murlis*, rather than existing scriptures. Also, they persisted in telling people that physical sex was impure, and that time repeated itself in an endless series of 5,000-year cycles. Worse, these heretical doctrines were being preached by women who were living independent lives and not marrying or having families. If the BKs were having a hard time in India, where the concepts of karma and reincarnation were at least accepted as fact, however would they survive in the West, which saw time as linear rather than cyclical, and regarded ideas about rebirth as so much nonsense?

READER/CUSTOMER CARE SURVEY

We care about your opinions. Please take a moment to fill out this Reader Survey card and mail it back to us.

As a special **"thank you"** we'll send you exciting news about interesting books and a valuable **Gift Certificate**

Please PRINT using ALL CAPITALS

BA1

Name
First ⊔ | Last
MI.⊔ | Name ⊔

Address ⊔

City ⊔ | ST ⊔ | Zip ⊔

Phone # (⊔ ⊔ ⊔) ⊔ ⊔ ⊔ - ⊔ ⊔ ⊔ ⊔ | Fax # (⊔ ⊔ ⊔) ⊔ ⊔ ⊔ - ⊔ ⊔ ⊔ ⊔

Email ⊔

(1) Gender:
○ Female
○ Male

(2) Age:
○ 13-19   ○ 40-49
○ 20-29   ○ 50-59
○ 30-39   ○ 60+

(3) Your children's age(s):
Please fill in all that apply.
○ 6 or Under   ○ 15-18
○ 7-10   ○ 19+
○ 11-14   or read?

(8) Marital Status:
○ Married
○ Single
○ Divorced / Widowed

(9) Was this book:
○ Purchased For Yourself?
○ Received As a Gift?

(10)How many HCI books have you bought or read?
○ 1   ○ 3
○ 2   ○ 4+

(11) Did this book meet your expectations?
○ Yes
○ No

(12) How did you find out about this book? *Please fill in ONE.*
○ Personal Recommendation
○ Store Display
○ TV/Radio Program
○ Bestseller List
○ Website
○ Advertisement/Article or Book
○ Catalog or Mailing
○ Other _____

(13) What FIVE subject areas do you enjoy reading about most? *Rank only FIVE. Choose 1 for your favorite, 2 for second favorite, etc.*

	1	2	3	4	5
Self Development	○	○	○	○	○
Parenting	○	○	○	○	○
Spirituality/Inspiration	○	○	○	○	○
Family and Relationships	○	○	○	○	○
Health and Nutrition	○	○	○	○	○
Recovery	○	○	○	○	○
Business/Professional	○	○	○	○	○
Entertainment	○	○	○	○	○
Sports	○	○	○	○	○
Teen Issues	○	○	○	○	○
Pets	○	○	○	○	○

FOLD HERE

BA1

9396058864

(25) Are you:
- ○ A Parent?
- ○ A Grandparent

(18) Where do you purchase most of your books?
Please fill in your top TWO choices only.
- ○ General Bookstore
- ○ Religious Bookstore
- ○ Warehouse / Price Club
- ○ Discount or Other Retail Store
- ○ Website
- ○ Book Club / Mail Order

(20) What type(s) of magazines do you SUBSCRIBE to?
Fill in up to FIVE categories.
- ○ Parenting
- ○ Sports
- ○ Fashion
- ○ Business / Professional
- ○ World News / Current Events
- ○ General Entertainment
- ○ Homemaking, Cooking, Crafts
- ○ Women's Issues
- ○ Other (please specify) _____

Also at that time, racism was rife in the UK and was to increase with the influx of large numbers of Ugandan Asians who came to Britain during the 1970s.

On arriving back in London, Jayanti felt that she would not so much have an uphill struggle as an impossible one. It was one thing for her mother to hold small social gatherings with other Indians in her home; quite another for her daughter to go out in her white sari and shawl and try to interest cynical worldly Westerners in these strange ideas.

"At first," Jayanti said, "we continued to meet in my mother's home. But although we expanded somewhat, the only people who were coming were Indians. However could I even hope to interest or attract any Westerners? In great fear and trepidation, I did start to contact little yoga groups offering to give lectures, talks and so on, but I got absolutely nowhere. Nobody was even remotely interested."

Jayanti believes now that her task, while difficult enough, would have been completely impossible but for her English education and upbringing.

There is no doubt in my mind that going to an English school, and mixing with English teenagers in the 1960s, made me far more streetwise and bold than I would otherwise have been. Even though I looked Indian, and wore the white sari, I had been socialized not to behave like a timid little Indian girl. As an Indian girl, I wouldn't even have been allowed to go out on my own, let alone knock on the doors of strange men—at least, not without a chaperone.

All the time that I seemed to be getting nowhere, Dadi Janki, still in India, was giving encouragement. She told me that there were soon to be big changes in the West, and that before long people would want to hear the message. I was not convinced but, emboldened by her positivity, I kept trying.

It was now the early 1970s and, looking back, I can see that Dadi was right. Throughout the 1950s and 1960s, people in the UK had been too comfortable to consider spiritual matters. They had warm homes, plenty of money—at least, compared to the majority in India—and safe jobs. There was universal free education, a free health service and everybody felt safe and secure. Why should they want to be interested in what sounded like a strange Indian cult where they were asked to give up all the good things in life, material things they had only just started to enjoy?

But towards the end of the 1960s major changes began to happen in the West, changes that Dadi Janki had foreseen. There were student protests; feminism was starting to become a powerful force, and young people were questioning all kinds of authority and institutions. Richard Hittleman had begun a yoga series on television which became surprisingly popular, and the Beatles became interested in transcendental meditation. The counter-culture was happening in California, and the hippie movement began, a movement of young people with rich parents. There was affluence to spare. People began taking drugs, and to become interested in altered states of consciousness. In America, people were beginning to explore their inner selves, and all kinds of consciousness-raising movements and institutions started.

For the first time in history, a critical number of people in the West had a high level of material comfort. It seems to me that you have to reach a certain level of material comfort before you can start to discover that material things don't satisfy every aspect of your needs. There was a wide spiritual chasm as more people began to question organized religion, and ever more people wanted to "do their own thing."

I had spent most of 1969 and 1970 knocking on doors, writing letters and getting nowhere, and I got very many doors slammed in my face. I think one major problem was that at the time all the so-called spiritual people I was trying to contact were men, and it was very unusual to have a young woman sharing spiritual concepts.

Jayanti's initial breakthrough came in 1970, at the Spiritualist Association of Great Britain, established since the 1930s in London's fashionable and expensive Belgrave Square. The Spiritualist Association has always firmly believed in rebirth and reincarnation, and the existence of souls as separate from bodies. Its members have all allegedly made contact with disembodied spirits, and meetings take the form of contacting those in the spirit world, for the benefit of their loved ones on Earth. Because they have never themselves easily fitted into the mainstream of Western religious or spiritual concepts, the Spiritualists have always been very open-minded about other faiths.

The then secretary of the association, Tom Johanson, had recently become interested in meditation, then a new concept in the West, and much derided, with the phrase "contemplating my navel" being used to discredit the practice. Tom had imposed on himself a year of silence as a spiritual discipline, and at the end of this year he had experienced a vision of God as a point of light—a vision that was similar to the Brahma Kumaris conception of God.

When Jayanti told him about the BK form of meditation, known as *raja yoga*, it connected with his own experience, and he was immediately interested in organizing a series of lectures at the association's central headquarters, so that people could listen to an expert on aspects of meditation.

"This was the starting point of our public lectures," Jayanti said. "People already interested in spiritual matters came to hear, and at last we had some kind of public platform. But, still, at the time I never thought there could ever be a center outside India."

Although physically very small like so many BKs (in fact, their small stature has prompted more than one person to ask if there is a height restriction if you wish to dedicate), Jayanti had one priceless asset, not possessed by any other BKs at the time, and that was a perfectly modulated, upper-class English accent. The socio-linguist John Honey has maintained that people can say the most outrageous things if they say them in a confident, pleasant, grammatical and accentless voice. The type of voice used actually gives, or reduces as the case may be, credibility, and people will stop and listen to you if you have an attractive, authoritative voice. It is perhaps knowing this that Dadi Janki has always chosen to speak through a translator when addressing public meetings in the West. Jayanti has always been easy to listen to, and this is a major reason why nowadays she is in great demand on public platforms all over the world. Her other great asset for furthering the BK cause in the West was that she also spoke fluent Hindi, so she could also act as interpreter.

In so many ways, she was the ideal person to bridge the gap between East and West, and enable the BKs to gain a foothold in the West.

In the spring of 1971, Dadi Janki told Jayanti that a delegation of BKs had been invited to a yoga conference in America, and they would be passing through London on the way. Five BKs were to be coming: Ramesh, Jagdish, Dr. Nirmala, Sister Rosie and Dadi Sheel. Dadi asked Jayanti if she might be able to organize some programs in London. She also mentioned the possibility of having a permanent center in London.

A small group offered to finance such a center and have a resident teacher from India to start the ball rolling. So the next step was to find suitable premises. "This was not at all easy," Jayanti said.

> For one thing, racism against Indians very much applied in the London of the early 1970s, and nobody wanted to give you accommodation. Because of my London upbringing, I sounded perfectly English on the phone, but discovered when I went to estate agents that places had mysteriously gone.
>
> But even without the racism, there was a major problem in finding a place where people would be allowed to come and go, and which at the same time would be close to my mother and myself. We had very little money to spare as well, so had to find somewhere cheap. Eventually we found an Indian landlord who actually wanted the place to be used for spiritual purposes. His previous tenant had been a pandit [an Indian wise or holy man], so in a way the place was prepared for us.

However, the very first Brahma Kumaris center in the West was hardly a palace. It was the downstairs flat in a tiny, dingy terraced house in northwest London.

Dr. Nirmala was appointed to be in charge of the new London center but soon she had to leave as she was needed elsewhere. So Dadi Ratan Mohini came to live at the little flat in Tennyson Road, northwest London. There were physical difficulties, as the flat was not even self-contained and the bathroom had to be shared with the other tenants upstairs. Also, Sister Ratan had never before even lived alone, or shared a bathroom with men.

As Jayanti delicately put it: "A lot of renunciation was needed." But gradually the little center started attracting regular meditators, and morning classes and meditation sessions began to be held every day.

Still, though, no Westerners had expressed any interest in hearing the teachings, although they had listened politely enough at the meetings held at the Spiritualist Association.

In April 1974 Dadi Janki finally agreed to leave India and come to London for three months to try and kick-start services in the West, and try to appeal to Westerners as well as Asians.

Dadi's view of her decision is that it happened entirely due to Jayanti's forcefulness and powers of persuasion, although she admits she had long thought that eventually she might be the one to take the message into the West. In 1974 Dadi Janki was aged fifty-eight, and Jayanti was twenty-five.

As soon as she knew for certain that Dadi was coming, Jayanti approached the Ceylon Tea Center and Indian Tea Center, to see if they could hold a pictorial exhibition there and advertise this. They agreed, and so the BKs had their first exhibitions in central London. These exhibitions showed pictures of the cycle, Indian gods and goddesses, the heavenly regions and other representations of BK teachings. Recalls Jayanti:

A lot of people came, as the exhibitions were unusual at the time, and there was very great interest, this time not just from Indians. Our first Westerners to show interest in our teachings came to these initial exhibitions. Because of this, which I must admit I had not anticipated, I felt we needed Dadi Janki here on a permanent basis to take things to a different level, and not just for three months.

Dadi had come to London with a group of other BKs which included Ramesh. At the time I was commuting between my mother's home and the Tennyson Road center, and Ramesh was put up as a lodger with the Afro-Caribbean family upstairs. Then the others had to go back, and Dadi Janki and I were left alone in Tennyson Road. I think we both knew in our hearts that Dadi was here to stay. Ratan Mohini returned to India.

Thus began the "dream team" of Dadi Janki and Jayanti, a partnership that remains as strong and fused as ever. Jayanti acted as Dadi's translator, as well as speaking at lectures in her own right whenever asked. It was not long before some Westerners began to appreciate the single-mindedness, dedication and sincerity of these two intelligent, intellectually rigorous and yet practical women, and to appreciate the spiritual concepts they were sharing.

Soon, a small group of Westerners started attending morning class and evening meditation regularly at the center. Two of the first to take the seven-day course, Denise Lawrence and John Kane, surrendered to become the first ever Western Brahma Kumaris in the UK.

In the early days, the Tennyson Road center was known as the Raja Yoga Center, and advertised itself as teaching "royal, or the highest form" of yoga. Many Westerners assumed this meant physical postures (*asanas*) and yogic breathing (*pranayama*) and were surprised to discover that the "yoga" was a form of open-eyed meditation rather than a way of contorting your body.

In fact, the Sanskrit word *yoga* means connection or tying, and has the same root as the Anglo-Saxon word *yoke*. In its original sense, the word yoga has nothing to do with exercises, although throughout the 1970s postural, or hatha, yoga became extremely popular in the West, and classes soon started up all over the country. Most hatha yoga classes included some easy spirituality and meditation, and thus a whole generation of people was introduced to Eastern concepts of peace, calm and mind/body harmony. Hatha yoga was a kind of "yoga without tears" as it did not require drastically altering your lifestyle.

But the Brahma Kumaris form of yoga was strongly disciplined, extremely uncompromising and needed constant effort and checking of the self. Some Westerners were attracted to the nonchanting, nonfussy form of meditation without incense, while others were intrigued by the exactness and logicality of the teachings, or body of knowledge. Others just liked to be near Dadi and Jayanti, and experience the strong vibrations of peace and love that they exuded.

Also, for those who came, the lack of commercialism was extremely refreshing, as was the non-guru aspect.

In December 1974, Denise Lawrence and another Westerner visited Madhuban, the very first Westerners ever to do so, and this was the start of foreigners coming there. Denise, a former hippie, soon started wearing a white sari and plaited her hair down her back, Indian-style. In the meantime, a subcenter had been started in Leicester by a small group of Ugandan Asians who had become interested in the teachings.

By the end of 1974 there were so many people coming to morning class and requesting the seven-day course that Dadi and Jayanti needed more personnel and more space. Sister Sudesh, who was later to become central to Western expansion of the organization, came over with another sister, to give classes and hold meditation sessions for the fast-increasing number of students, both Western and Indian. The original flat, consisting of two downstairs rooms and a kitchen in a very small terraced house, was now far too small to accommodate all the students. They needed to find new premises fast—and before long, had a piece of luck.

"By early 1975 the house next door to our flat had become vacant, and we made the decision to purchase it," Jayanti said. "We now had a whole house, with upstairs and downstairs which, although still small, was at least ours. And at least we no longer had to share a bathroom or sleep on the floor, as previously."

Until the house was purchased, Dadi Janki, at the age of nearly sixty, was not only living in a rather rough and certainly working-class area of London, but was sleeping on a wooden plank and sharing a none-too-clean bathroom with strangers. At the time she did not speak or understand a word of English and had been, since her earliest years, in very poor health, liable to sudden, devastating and serious illnesses.

Now here she was, in a cold, strange, alien land, not speaking the language, not fitting in anywhere, and living in bleak comfortless accommodation. But she was not unhappy, for she was at last embarking on her life's work, the work she had envisioned twenty years previously.

And, it seemed, the West was finally ready to hear and take to its heart the message of the Brahma Kumaris.

A PERSONAL STORY

It was in early 1981 that my then husband Neville and I first came into contact with the Brahma Kumaris or, as they were known in the West in those days, the Raj Yogis. At the time I was working for a notorious British newspaper, the Rupert Murdoch-owned *Sun*. Neville had recently left his job as medical correspondent for the *Daily Mail* to write a book about mind-body medicine. Neither paper was much given to spirituality and neither were we, although we had recently put a tiny little toe into the exotic and then quite unfamiliar waters of Eastern-based spiritual movements by attending a weekend organized by the Siddha Yoga group, headed by the Indian guru Swami Muktananda.

Siddha yoga, along with a number of other Eastern spiritual groups, was fast becoming popular in the West and the

weekend was rather off-puttingly hosted by Westerners wearing the robes, and adopting the demeanor, of Indian holy
men. They were Western enough to take our Visa cards on
entry, though, and advise us that refreshments were extra, on
top of the price for the nonresidential weekend intensive.

I had hated that weekend with a mighty passion. Not only
was it extremely expensive, but the chanting and the meditation were pure unadulterated agony. I had never attempted to
meditate before and my first experience of turning inwards
and trying to still my mind had the exact opposite effect of the
one intended. I felt extremely peaceless during the lengthy
sessions, all the more so as all around me people were
writhing, rocking to and fro, making anguished sounds and
snorting, coughing and spluttering. And this went on for
hours. It felt extremely alien, and there seemed something
spurious about it, although I could not put my finger on
exactly what. Certainly it was not an experience I wished to
repeat.

Neville did not want to attend any more such weekends
either, but something that had happened to him some
months previously had made him wonder whether there
might be more to life than eating, sleeping, writing newspaper stories and drinking wine in the evenings.

As medical correspondent for a popular daily newspaper, he
was always being sent press releases announcing this or that
important event or astonishing medical breakthrough. Most of
these pieces of paper went straight into the wastepaper basket,
and one that might have followed its fellows into the bin was
an invitation to a press conference at Westminster Abbey
hosted by the Dean of Westminster, Dr. Edward Carpenter.

Neville felt himself far too busy working on proper stories to bother with this kind of thing.

However, on the morning of the event, a doctor contact telephoned him to try to persuade him to go. He was not keen, yet when the time came for the press conference, something made him decide to give it the benefit of the doubt. The dean and his guest, an Indian religious teacher, both spoke about their concepts of the soul and the press conference finished with a meditation in which the swami's followers chanted a mantra to do with God Shiva. In the silence that followed, a most peculiar thing happened. Neville went into a state of altered consciousness, in which he saw a golden-red light and experienced for the first time a sensation of peace and bliss. Although at the time he was an extremely hard-headed and even ruthless journalist, not readily given to flights of fancy, he could not deny the reality of that experience.

And, as when anything really wonderful happens, he was keen to repeat the experience, which was one reason we had attended the siddha yoga weekend. But nothing did happen, nothing positive anyway, and gradually it all faded into the background, while normal life, or what passed for it, resumed.

Neville, however, was unable to forget his visionary experience, and had started to investigate different kinds of meditation with a view to writing an article on the subject. One day while attending a medical meeting, he met a young woman who talked extremely enthusiastically about the Brahma Kumaris, a new yoga movement she had come across which was run by women. She was twenty-three-year-old Jenny Pusey, who had traveled round India after university seeking enlightenment, and had eventually found it not in the East, but on her own doorstep, in London, with the BKs. She invited him to meet some members of this group who, she said, would be able to answer his questions much more effectively than she could. Because of the women's angle, Neville mentioned this encounter to me, wondering whether I might be able to do something on the BKs for one of the many women's magazines I contributed to at the time, as well as working for the *Sun*.

I was intrigued, as I had never before come across a spiritual group headed by women, and I contacted Eric Bailey, editor of *She* magazine, then an avant-garde, irreverent publication, for whom I did regular work. The twin aspects of women being at the head, and of never charging fees for any events, made this group sound worthy of a write-up, I thought, and Eric, always interested in bizarre byways of human conduct, agreed.

He commissioned me to write a piece, so I arranged for myself and Neville to meet members of the Brahma Kumaris one evening after work at a center they had in Richmond, Surrey, just down the road from where we were then living.

This center was a small modern house in a new residential development, furnished simply and in neutral colors. Inside the house were four women, Jayanti, Sudesh, Veronica McHugh, a young Irish woman who had surrendered about four years previously, and Jenny Pusey. All were wearing white saris, which made them look impossibly holy, compared to myself, and I felt unaccountably awe-stricken as I took off my shoes and sat opposite them on a sofa.

After I had heard enough for a 1,000-word introductory article, I shut my notebook, believing that would be that, apart from fixing up pictures. But then the sisters asked if

Neville and I would like to try their method of meditation. Okay, I agreed out of politeness, why not? Jayanti explained that we should keep our eyes open, fixing our gaze on the "third eye" or point between the forehead, of one of the sisters. We settled ourselves into meditation mode and soft Indian-type music played, above which Jayanti spoke a commentary to help us direct and focus our minds on peace and tranquillity, while Sudesh sat in front of us.

The commentary went something like this:

> *I, the soul, am a pure peaceful point of light . . . a tiny point of energy . . . I am now turning my thoughts inward to the self, the soul, in the center of my forehead . . . this physical body is only a costume . . . which I, the living energy use . . . it exists for me to express my being, my personality.*
>
> *Now I realize my true identity . . . I have unlocked the gate to my true nature . . . I am now free, like a bird, to fly.*
>
> *I now emerge my true nature, which is peace . . . I now experience that peace . . . I am that peace . . . I experience my true nature, that of light . . . I become that light . . . I experience my true nature . . . that of love . . . I become that love . . . I am that love.*
>
> *Now I am filling the soul with power . . . lightness and ease become my nature . . . now I am no longer the slave, but the master of this body . . . I become able to spread light and purity into the world.*

Everybody sat very still during this meditation, and there was no chanting, no mantra, no ritual and no writhing or spluttering. We sat meditating for about five or ten minutes, and then the session was over. There were no dramatic meditational experiences for me, although Neville told me that he had experienced an intense feeling of spiritual power radiating from Sudesh. We both agreed that we had experienced a potent feeling of calm, and also the very strong conviction that this group was completely genuine and a force for good.

Because we had seemed so interested in what the sisters were saying, not just for a magazine article, but for ourselves, they asked whether we would like to take their seven-day course to find out more about the organization and its beliefs. We looked at each other and, for some reason, agreed. After all, the sisters seemed sensible and intelligent, the center was only just down the road, and there were no fees or charges. Also, we might even learn something, you never knew.

Then, before we finally left, Jayanti gave us both a piece of *toli*, an Indian homemade sweet. It tasted of condensed milk and pistachio, and I rather liked it.

Thus it was that we embarked on the seven-day course with Veronica, known as Waddy (Indians couldn't pronounce Veronica, she told us, and this was the nearest they could get to her name), as our teacher. There was nobody actually living at this center at the time, but Veronica came over from the main center especially for our classes. The house belonged to Jayanti and was her "dowry," donated to the Brahma Kumaris by her father when he realized that his daughter was never going to get married.

Before long, Neville and I were joined by Erin Pizzey, then very famous for establishing refuges for battered women, and her young American husband Jeff Shapiro, twenty-one years Erin's junior.

The four of us had endless questions, so many that our supposed seven-day course lasted three months. Erin was Catholic, Jeff was Jewish, Neville and I came from Protestant backgrounds, although we had long both been practicing atheists, so we made a fine old mixture between us. Erin was intense, Neville was logical and scientific, and Jeff and I were just intrigued.

None of us had any problems with the notions that all of us want peace, happiness, stability, love and contentment, good relationships with others, and to be optimistic and cheerful rather than pessimistic and depressed. I had recently read the book *Your Erroneous Zones*, by Dr. Wayne Dyer, which made the point that we can actually choose whether to be angry, happy, sad or resentful. That book came as a revelation to me and now here were these same ideas being presented in a spiritual context.

Nor did any of us have trouble with the notion that nowadays most people are full of the five vices of anger, greed, ego, lust and attachment. Of these five vices, ego was by far the worst, we were advised, as it informed all the other vices, and had many subtle offshoots. Ego, which was false pride, had to be distinguished from genuine self-esteem and self-confidence. The meditation practice would, we were told, in time enable us to root out elements of the five vices in ourselves, and allow the soul's true nature to emerge, which was that of peace.

Anger was also a dangerous vice and we could, with practice, actually choose not to feel anger. If we felt insulted by something somebody had said, that was our problem rather than theirs. We should try to feel nothing but benevolence towards others, as if they do wrong that is their ignorance and we should feel sorry for them. Everybody, even Hitler, the BKs said, believes they are doing right, or at least the best they can, even when the general consensus is that they are evil.

Through regular meditation and turning inwards, we heard, we would learn to distinguish and discriminate between good and bad actions in ourselves. We should never judge others, but should always be the harshest critics of ourselves, we learned, and make sure our own actions are guided by the very best motives. Harboring bad thoughts and resentments about others only does ourselves harm. It may not even affect the others, but it will certainly disturb our own peace of mind.

All four of us enjoyed these "positive thinking" aspects of the course, and we also appreciated the peaceful, calm atmosphere which pervaded the little house during our sessions there.

It was when we came to the more contentious aspects of the teachings, those concerning celibacy, the cycle and consciousness, or the Three Cs, that the questions and objections started. Neville purported to find much of what was being said here as going right against modern scientific findings, and Erin and Jeff were not happy with the insistence on celibacy for those wishing to connect to a higher source. The idea that Brahma Baba had, on death, somehow joined with God himself was difficult for any of us to come to terms with as well, although the Christian teaching that Jesus joined with God after his death on the cross was not so very different, in some ways. But that all happened thousands of years ago, whereas

Brahma Baba was a modern man, a businessman, not somebody who had long ago become part of myth and legend.

But as time went on, and we became more familiar with the ideas, I found that I, at least, could accept most of them without too much trouble.

Their views on celibacy sounded interesting, especially as they were in direct contradiction to the prevailing orthodoxy about sex, which maintained that physical sex could be a spiritual, transcendent experience in itself. Indeed one guru, Bhagwan Shree Rajneesh, had encouraged his followers to take part in multiple sexual orgies for the sake of spiritual enlightenment.

It seemed that sex, rather than religion, had become the opium of the people, but already rumblings of discontent were starting, mainly from American radical feminists who were questioning the new centrality of physical sex. Andrea Dworkin was saying that no woman needs sex, although few avoid it, and an American publication, *The Celibate Woman*, had just come into being. The BK view was a spiritual version of a similar viewpoint, and held that women — and men — can actually have better, more equal relationships with each other when sexual desire or attraction is not present. Their uncompromising stand against sex was that it is overwhelmingly an expression of body-consciousness, and that sexual desire can easily call up all the other vices.

Of course, none of us knew at the time how vital celibacy had been to the establishment of the Om Mandali, how it had been both their greatest problem and their greatest strength, and how it had led to court cases, torture, ill treatment, assassination attempts and adverse publicity. As we did not then know the whole background to the organization, we were a little surprised at the vehemence of their anti-sex stand.

At first I found it strange that they were advocating celibacy for married as well as single people, as on marriage one was generally considered to sign up for sex for life. It was part and parcel of the marriage contract, in the East as well as the West. But then I thought: *Why should it be? Why does everlasting sex have to be built into the contract?* It then came home to me that most people did not have a perceived choice about whether or not to engage in sexual activity. We had been brought up to consider it natural, and if there was distaste for it, that was seen as our fault for being frigid or having a low sex drive, rather than that there could be anything wrong with sex itself.

I also found the BK views on time and evolution logical and sensible, and appreciated the linked concepts of karma and reincarnation, especially as they were being clearly explained for the first time. The idea that we are all responsible for our actions and that nothing happens in a vacuum was comforting and reassuring. Suddenly, much that had previously bothered me about the unfairness and injustice of life began to make sense, now that I was being given some understanding as to how injustices come about. They are caused by past karma, rather than being random events. I also liked the idea that nothing goes unnoticed and that every action has its direct consequence, for good or ill.

As the BKs explained it, human life was not random and pointless, but all part of an elaborate interlinked pattern. Because we cannot see the pattern, we should not assume it is not there. Everything happens for a reason, we were told, and it all takes place accurately according to the "drama," even though it may not seem like it at the time. Everything is "meant," and everything that takes place is another piece that fits into the vast interlocking jigsaw of our many incarnations.

And because every action counts, we ourselves must be careful never to cause sorrow, never to set bad karma in motion, and never to imagine that our sins will not find us out. The doctrine of karma, as explained by the BKs, is not one of crime and punishment, but of inevitable cause and effect. It is not God who "allows" bad things to happen, but humans who bring them about by their actions when influenced by lust, anger and ego.

If I am born in poor circumstances, they explained, that is not a punishment by God, but a consequence of past actions carried through to the next physical costume. Similarly, if I am born into wealth and privilege, that too is a result of past karma.

We asked, of course: What exactly is it that reincarnates? The answer was that it is the soul, the eternal, non-dimensional and nonphysical aspect of ourselves. And the soul consists of three elements: the mind, the intellect and behavioral tendencies or predispositions, known as *sanskars*. The mind, we were told, was not an aspect of the physical brain, but of the nonphysical soul. As to *when* a new soul incarnates, the BKs had an exact answer to that as well. This enters the body of an unborn baby at about four months' gestation, or when the first quickening is noticed. When somebody dies, the BK understanding is that his or her soul leaves the body, enters another almost immediately, and begins a new life about five months later.

The course explained that we have all had the sensation, when meeting somebody new, that we have known them all our lives. Conversely, other people may remain eternal strangers, so that we find we never click with them at all. These are examples of karma. In the first case, there is most probably some joint karma, some unfinished business between us; in the second case, there is no such connection, therefore no mutual interest in each other. The longer souls go back, the more karma they will have accumulated.

Although, in BK understanding, the 5,000-year cycle repeats identically every time; this does not mean we do not have choice and free will. For instance, it may be in the "drama" that I will become a doctor or lawyer, but I will still have to work to pass exams. We always have to make effort; there is never an excuse for complacency. Also, as I do not know the future, I have to act as though it were happening for the first time.

The way to regard the "drama" of our lives is as though we are watching it happen, and to understand that we are not just the roles we play. We must appreciate that nothing lasts forever, that all material things are impermanent, and that if we have good luck today, we may have bad luck tomorrow, and vice versa. There is no way of ensuring material security, but if we have the awareness of watching everything unfold, as if a spectator, we can start to lose attachment to our roles. We are not mothers, fathers, doctors, husbands, judges, insurance clerks: These are only temporary roles we may be playing for a short time in the great scheme of things. When we take on another bodily costume, these roles may be very different.

In the meantime, we should do all we can—aided by daily

meditation—to remain calm and positive; to treat every happening as a challenge and a learning experience, but never to lose our equilibrium.

The BKs soon gave us a practical experience of this attitude. During our course, a public event had been arranged at the Richmond Center, where our friends and contacts could hear an introduction to the BKs. Two sisters and Dadi Janki (who at this stage none of us had met) were coming over in a car from Willesden, northwest London, to give a talk and meditation experience. Around thirty people had come to hear the program, which was to begin at 7:30.

Seven thirty came and went. Eight o'clock came and went. Quarter past eight. We had heard of Indian time, but this was starting to get ridiculous. One of us rang the Willesden Center, to be told that the sisters had certainly set out on time. Where were they? This was, of course, before the days of mobile phones, which all BKs now have. Eventually, a phone call came to say they had broken down, and Neville set out in his car to try and find them. He discovered them a few miles away, waiting by the side of the road. But instead of being consumed with anxiety, they were all sitting calmly meditating and smiling, perfectly content.

When Neville expressed astonishment at their lack of fluster, they replied: "We knew you would come for us. In any case, it's a chance for us to have a ride in your car."

As I listened to the course, I felt I had never heard spiritual ideas explained so clearly and rationally. Christianity, with its strange psychicism, its insistence that we believe the patently impossible, such as the Virgin Birth, had never appealed to me. Also, Christians had no way of explaining why there is so much injustice in the world. To say simply that "It's God's will" is not enough. But here, we were being told that humans create their own world, their own systems; it is nothing to do with God, who does not cause or create injustice and inequality. In fact, these things happen only when we start to forget God, and the spiritual dimension of life.

Once we can link ourselves back to God through yoga, then we can start remembering ourselves as pure, peaceful, loveful souls once more. Gradually, as we meditate, our old attachments fade away, ego and arrogance are dissolved, and our true nature, which is that of benevolence, kindness and love, can flourish.

The BKs have a favorite slogan, which can be found displayed in many of their centers: *When we change, the world changes.* During the course, we heard that if we want to set major reforms in motion we must always start with ourselves, work from the inside out rather than the outside in. The Om Mandali had begun life as a self-transformation group and only when the members felt themselves powerful enough did external service begin.

In order to re-emerge positive qualities, we heard, strict lifestyle disciplines are needed. We must separate ourselves from our addictions, desires and attachments, from the bodily vices developed over many incarnations. Dedicated members of the Brahma Kumaris all rise at 4:00 A.M. to meditate. They do this every single day of the year, in all parts of the world. This silent meditation, known as *amrit vela,* or the early hours of nectar, sets us up for the rest of the day in the right spirit.

Early morning meditation is followed by the reading of that day's *murli,* and a class given by a senior sister, held at a BK center. This all finishes at around eight in the morning, when the working day begins. But at intervals throughout the day BKs will also observe "traffic control": a couple of minutes of silent meditation to still and calm the mind. There is also a group meditation session at each center in the evenings. On Thursdays, "Baba's day," the class is longer, and refreshments, or *brahma bhojan* are handed out.

It has been said by Christians that cleanliness is next to godliness, and this is certainly observed by the BKs. The strictest attention is paid to personal cleanliness and hygiene, and the level of cleanliness of their centers is not so much an absence of dirt, as an actual shining quality. In the words of George Herbert's hymn, they "make drudgery divine," as everything they do is in the name of Baba. Therefore (in theory at least) the lowest tasks are as important as the highest ones. If done in God's remembrance, there is no such thing as a lowly task.

All food has to be prepared and eaten in Baba's remembrance and because of this BKs will not eat food prepared by non-BKs. They adhere to a strict vegetarian diet and exclude onions and garlic, as these have the reputation of exciting sexual lust. They do not eat eggs, as these are embryonic animals and also the sulphur in them can, apparently, excite sex-lust.

BKs are not encouraged to read novels or go to the cinema or theater, although Brahma Baba did urge members of the Om Mandali to read one newspaper a day, so that they would know what was going on in the world. The sisters do not wear make-up and dedicated members wear only white.

We were told that some BKs continued with their everyday,

or *lokik*, jobs while others ran centers full-time. The vastly simplified way of life meant that they could live extremely cheaply. They did not go on holiday or vacation as such, although all made an annual pilgrimage to Madhuban. Dedicated, or surrendered, members had no personal possessions, and regarded all money they might earn as "Baba's money." If they owned a house, it was considered Baba's house. In this way, they lived much like traditional monks or nuns.

While we were all impressed with the way the dedicated members managed to practice what they preached, when first presented to us the lifestyle sounded bleak and unexciting, impossibly austere. I did not imagine I could ever give up my love of make-up and fashionable clothes, and I could simply not envisage a life devoid of novels. Reading was one of my greatest passions, and I also enjoyed theater, cinema, wine, dinner parties, nights out, social occasions, gossiping. But then we were told: Take what you can. Extreme dedication is not for everybody.

As the four of us continued to listen intently to what was being said, it was clear that we were having very different reactions. Erin and Jeff found the stark simple lifestyle difficult to imagine (Erin was writing *The Slut's Cookbook* at the time) and Neville was mortally offended by the BK concepts of evolution and how things began, concepts that contradicted Darwinism at every turn. To Neville the ideas, or body of revealed knowledge, as the BKs saw it, were unscientific, unproven, naïve, creationist, childish.

He argued and argued. If everything goes round in such short cycles, he objected, what about fossils? What about dinosaurs? What about hominids, whose bones have been found? What about links between apes and man? When we were told quite seriously that dinosaurs, fossils and such might be the results of a planetary upheaval at the end of the previous cycle, Neville found it laughable. The BKs believe—and this doctrine can also be found in some ancient scriptures— that each 5,000-year cycle ends with the bang of a full-scale nuclear holocaust. There is also the concept, held by some BKs, that dinosaurs and such strange animals are short-lasting mutants from the fallout, rather than creatures roaming the primeval swamp for millions of years, as evolutionists hold.

Some people, though, will survive the holocaust and become the new Golden Aged people. Then the new age will begin, with peace, prosperity, plenty, and the whole process will start once more. To underline their point, the BKs reminded us that it is in the nature of things to start out new and grow old. Factories do not manufacture old goods, but new ones. Humans do not start out as old people, but tiny babies. Why should planet Earth be any different? Also, in support of the concept of cyclical time, the same point was made: In nature, everything is cyclical, by its very nature. Which, they asked, comes first, the seed or the tree?

The weather during the Golden Age is perpetually that of late spring, we heard, as the Earth changes slightly on its axis during this time.

We are now, we were told, in the Confluence Age, the time where the old Iron Age is ready to die out. "Realized souls" will usher in this new age. Of course, many religious and spiritual movements have proclaimed that the end of the world is nigh, and these predictions have been going on since

Anglo-Saxon times at least. They are rife in Western medieval literature, and are commonly dismissed as means to make the ignorant sit up and pay attention. But maybe there is something in them, especially as most religions say the same, or a similar, thing.

Neville found it all far too much to be asked to accept. Yet he had already developed a huge respect for these endearing white-clad women, and enjoyed their constant equanimity— a quality he felt singularly lacking in himself. And in spite of his aggressive questioning, whenever it came time for the meditation, he would go off into a different realm and experience aspects of that same bliss and peace as when in Westminster Abbey. If the dramatic lights and mental fireworks were not there, his ability to experience another reality continued, and made him keep going back for more, in spite of his inability to grasp many aspects of the teachings. Eventually, the yearning to find out more made him want to go regularly to the main center.

My own experience in meditation was nothing so strong, and after our prolonged course finally ended, Erin, Jeff and I faded away, while Neville's involvement became ever stronger.

At home, things got so serious that we started to observe some of the BK precepts, such as vegetarianism and celibacy. We found these an interesting diversion from our previous habits, and they had the effect of promoting exciting, sometimes painful, discoveries about ourselves and the ways in which we related to each other. We discovered that life without sex was not only possible but even enjoyable, and that a vegetarian diet definitely had a positive effect on anger and aggression levels.

Neville went even further and gave up all alcohol and most social occasions. He now started to find dinner parties trivial and pointless, and had ever less inclination to go to the cinema or watch television. He also gave up golf and sold his golf clubs. In a sense, it was not so much that he gave up these activities and interests as that they began to be less appealing to him, compared with meditating and reading the *murlis*, which before long became almost his only reading matter.

He discovered in himself a new calmness, self-confidence and serenity, believing that in the past much of his frenetic activity had been motivated by fear, and a sensation of emptiness inside. He began to be convinced that meditation was the best medicine, and built this into his daily life. Of course, friends and family who were observing him closely expected him to become instantly perfect, and were disappointed whenever his halo started slipping, not realizing, or at least not accepting, that self-transformation takes many years of hard work.

For three years, Neville stayed away from his well-paid newspaper job in order to devote more time to his spiritual study, as well as to write a book. The simplified way of life we had now embarked on made this financially possible, and we managed to live quite well on what I earned as a journalist and author.

As time went on, the BKs were amused at the difference between Neville and myself. While I had no difficulty in accepting the body of knowledge, even their theories about dinosaurs and fossils (never having found either of the remotest interest, I couldn't really care less about how they came into being), I continued to find meditation boring and tedious. Neville, by contrast, who could not accept so many elements of the knowledge, or *gyan*, was increasingly finding it difficult to go for even a day without meditating.

And so our way of life changed forever, thanks to the BKs. We moved and Neville turned our basement into a mini-BK center, complete with a picture of Brahma Baba. Every week-day morning a few people would turn up at our house for a yoga class. On one evening a week about two dozen BKs would come to our house for class and meditation, led by a senior sister. Neville made a number of trips to Madhuban and, eventually, felt that he had found the answer to the meaning of life. He fell in love with the movement, became a dedicated BK. He wanted me to go along with all this, but I could not, much as I liked the organization, and much as I had appreciated the teachings and hearing another perspective on life.

I now believe that, in order to become a BK, you have to experience something akin to falling in love. You have to *feel* passionately the truth of what is being said; you cannot take it on board only by using logic and reason. The intellect is not strong enough on its own to pull you towards these beliefs, quell all your doubts and enable you to relinquish all the "good" things in life, to separate yourself from your previous wicked ways.

Neville's friends and family thought, of course, that he had been brainwashed by a mysterious, witch-like cult of exotic, seductive women, and waited for him to come to his senses. Everybody had by now heard of "love-bombing," the technique by which certain non-mainstream cults bombard new recruits with love and gifts, to gain their undying allegiance, before taking all their money from them. Some people assumed the BKs were like this, and that a day of reckoning would come when Neville was helplessly in their clutches, unable to think for himself.

But that day of reckoning never happened. The BKs never demanded anything of him, and Neville became ever more firmly convinced that the BK teachings were correct and accurate, and had far more power of truth than any others he had ever heard. If he still had some doubts, he put them on one side for the time being. Instead of running a BK center, though, which he had at one time considered, he went back to full-time work, as medical and science correspondent of the *Sunday Times*. Nevertheless, a few years later we decided to separate, as our lifestyles were now becoming too widely divergent for it to be possible to live together any more. We sold the Richmond house, and moved into separate accommodation.

We had started to feel that our relationship had come to an end in its present form, and that it was time to redefine it as one of friends rather than marital partners. In fact, during the end of our time together many visitors to our house assumed we were brother and sister, even though there is not the remotest physical likeness between us. But we were just not like the standard married couple, they told us.

Although I did not hear the call to dedicate and become a fully fledged BK, I remained on friendly terms and watched the organization progress. Meanwhile, Erin and Jeff left the country to live abroad.

By the time Neville and I first came into contact with the BKs in 1981, they had already moved on considerably from their humble beginnings in Tennyson Road. They now had a large, well-appointed house in St. Gabriel's Road, Willesden, where classes, programs and early morning meditation were held. They still owned the little house in Tennyson Road, and some classes continued to be held there, as in the early days.

But now there were several dozen centers dotted around the UK. The university had also expanded into other Western countries. Australian service, under the aegis of Dr. Nirmala, was thriving, and there were also several centers in North and South America. Denise Lawrence, one of the first Westerners to dedicate, was now running a center in San Francisco and before long Veronica left the UK to start a center in Tampa.

The university had started to hold major programs in London, hiring halls seating several thousand people, and celebrities were invited to speak at these. Again, no charges were ever made for the conferences, which were extremely successful and on such themes as the environment, inner peace, spiritual education and feminism. I remember the ecologist Teddy Goldsmith, actor Bill Roache (of the British soap *Coronation Street*) and former Westminster School headmaster John Rae taking those early platforms. Nobody, it seemed, minded being associated with the Brahma Kumaris, even though most celebrity speakers felt it difficult to take on board the whole package of their beliefs.

One doctor spoke disparagingly of "ill-fitting Eastern ideologies," and, at the time, many professional people felt that the uncompromising Indianness of the BKs could not be successfully welded on to current Western thought and behavior. There were far too many points of divergence and also a wide, uncrossable cultural gap, many people considered.

Yet throughout the early 1980s the BKs were managing to attract ever more Westerners. By 1984, there were at least as

many Western as Indian members in the UK, and in countries such as Australia and Germany there were virtually no
Indians at all.

They were also holding large international conferences on
peace issues at their Madhuban headquarters, to which they
managed to attract world-class speakers. One year Jehan
Sadat, widow of the assassinated Egyptian President Anwar
Sadat, shared a platform with Edward Carpenter, Dean of
Westminster Abbey. Labor politician Lord Ennals, a member
of Harold Wilson's cabinet, also went to speak at a major
Madhuban conference, eventually becoming very close to
the university.

Madhuban itself had considerably expanded, and in 1983
they built the Universal Peace Hall, which could hold 3,000
people. Thousands of Westerners were now coming every
year, from all over the world; some staying at Madhuban for
months on end.

Even with such expansion, nobody ever asked for fees or
charges and although contributions were always welcomed,
they were never requested, as every visitor to Madhuban was
considered to be a "guest" of the university. No doubt some
people exploited the generosity of the Brahma Kumaris, but
in their history very few have ever taken advantage. It seems
as though the boundless generosity, the philosophy of giving
rather than taking, actually makes people behave better than
they normally might.

By the mid-1980s, senior sisters such as Dadi Janki were
themselves being invited to attend conferences held by the
United Nations and other world organizations. They were
becoming recognized as a force for good all over the world

although, as ever, they kept an extremely low profile. Although now in demand for her wisdom and insights on many current issues, Dadi Janki always firmly resisted any adulation or worship for herself, and never sought attention. Nor did any of the other BKs, as they were only too aware of the subtle pull of ego should they accept any special treatment for themselves.

The first Western married couple to surrender jointly, in the early 1980s, were David and Maureen Goodman, a young couple from the north of England. Maureen came to live permanently in London to help run the Willesden Center and, in common with other Western surrendered sisters, she adopted the white sari.

I think one of the things that kept me friendly and positive towards the BKs while my previous way of life was in such momentous upheaval was their sense of humor. It is not always easy to translate humor from one culture to another, but I discovered that most of the people who were attracted to the BKs were fond of jokes, laughter, being sent up. Even Baba's *murlis*, the discourses apparently delivered by God himself through his bodily medium, were full of humor and laughter. And though the BKs led such a strictly disciplined life themselves, there was nothing grim or harsh or off-puttingly earnest about them. They also always attended closely to the physical comfort of their guests, in the belief that it is difficult to experience spiritual peace if your body is in extreme discomfort.

Another refreshing aspect was that they always invited discussion and debate, and wanted to hear all sides. They often asked people who emphatically did not share their views to come and speak at their programs and events. This was in direct contrast to many Eastern-based organizations which, at least in the 1980s, invited you to leave "your shoes and your mind at the door." Muslims, Christians, atheists, anthropologists, physicists, doctors and other professionals, often holding views directly opposed to those of the BKs, came to speak at their programs. The idea was always: Let's see whether we have any points of contact, so that we can maybe work together to improve the future for all of us.

There was also, I discovered, much individuality among BKs themselves. Jayanti was intellectually rigorous, Dadi Janki was, in her unassuming way, an extremely radical feminist; Sudesh was an inspired teacher of meditation; Waddy and Maureen were warm-hearted and approachable. Neville, everybody thought, was "extremely British," whatever that meant.

Each member brought his or her own unique qualities to the organization. The young men who were being attracted helped the organization to expand in many ways. Some gifted musicians were now BKs, and they helped develop the use of music as a meditation aid. Other Western men redesigned and rewrote the literature to make it more accessible to Westerners. Some had building, design or lighting skills, and the look of the centers started to improve as they lost their "Indianness" and became more appealing to Westerners.

An early difficulty which both Neville and I had was in knowing the difference between what was God's *shrimat,* or holy directions, and what was, in fact, merely Indian custom. Nowadays, this bothers people much less, as the BKs have themselves become far more Western. As one member said:

"We've had to learn from you how to be Western. At first, we had no idea. We didn't know what Westerners wanted, or what they might accept."

The challenge of not compromising their beliefs or way of life, while at the same time modernizing and Westernizing themselves, is one that has constantly exercised the movement ever since it gained a foothold in Western countries.

Their eventual breathtaking success in this endeavor was only just round the corner, and will be described in the following chapters.

FIVE

THE UN
CONNECTION

At the same time as Dadi Janki and Jayanti were working together to establish a solid BK base in Britain, interesting things began to happen in America when another remarkable female duo, Mohini Panjabi and Gayatri Naraine, joined forces.

And in the same way that Dadi and Jayanti were exactly right for the UK, Mohini and Gayatri were just the people to preside over America, thus neatly illustrating the BK maxim that everything that happens is "accurate" and dovetails neatly according to the drama.

For whereas Dadi and Jayanti are inspirational and, in a way, timeless, Mohini and Gayatri are more modern. Both are educated, sophisticated women who have also held down contemporary careers: Mohini as a political journalist and

Gayatri as a university administrative official. Their brisk, no-nonsense style is perhaps more suited to fast-moving America as Dadi and Jayanti's fluid, organic and also rigorously intellectual methods fit more easily into the old world.

Also, Mohini and Gayatri both came from diplomatic, rather than business, families which gave them the ideal background for the diplomatic role they were destined to adopt in New York.

Originally it was thought that Mohini would settle in London, and she did indeed live in the dingy little downstairs flat in Tennyson Road for a while where, as Jayanti had put it "much renunciation was needed." But after Dadi Janki arrived in the UK, Mohini—as one of the rare English-speaking BKs at the time—was needed elsewhere. There were just not enough key personnel in those early days to be able to crowd all the senior sisters into London.

Mohini, a large Indian woman with a beautiful smile, describes how she first came into contact with the BKs, and what inspired her finally to dedicate her life to the movement:

> *I first met the BKs in 1951 when I was eleven years old. In 1950, when they first came to India from Pakistan, some of them knew my grandfather, who worked in government. In fact, most of my family were in government service, and several BK sisters came to our house in Delhi to see if my grandfather could help with certain services.*
>
> *In those days it was difficult to get a telephone connection, and also at that time, just after independence and the bloody struggles that followed, food was rationed. There were around 300 people in Mount Abu at the time, and not*

enough to eat. My grandfather was happy to help out in any way he could, but he remained clear on one thing: that he did not want our family to become involved with the BKs on a deeper level.

But when I saw them, I strongly felt their purity. I felt, even at that age, that they were very different from ordinary people. They seemed very simple and very beautiful, and I was fascinated by them, especially as most of them were women, and it was unusual then to see women in leadership roles.

Gradually, as I grew up, I became ever more interested. We were a big extended family living in Delhi, and there were about thirty or forty of us, each with our own quarters. When I was about fifteen, I decided to write a letter to Brahma Baba in Mount Abu, and that led to some communication between us. The Delhi Center at the time was about fifteen minutes' walk away from my home, and the sisters invited us to attend. I went along, and what attracted me at the time was that the package was very simple yet extremely dedicated. It seemed to me that the truth was being taught, and this was very visible in the way they lived and conducted themselves.

My family had several gurus, and used to go on pilgrimages to shrines and holy places. But I had never felt that kind of fascination with gurus and holy men. I never felt that I could ever be part of that kind of devotion.

Then in 1957 Brahma Baba came to Delhi and I met him for the first time. I was so impressed with him, and with the whole BK set-up. Everything was so clean, so well-organized, and I felt that the BK life was a very good one.

My family went to the center as well, but after a time they stopped as they began to be afraid of the ways that the Brahma Kumaris teachings differed from traditional Hinduism. They felt they could not give up their gurus and their worship, ritual and devotion. Also, I think that my family were extremely concerned that I might become a BK myself.

It was understood that a woman's life was her family, and nobody ever thought that some woman might not want this kind of life for herself. It was not expected that a woman might not want a family, and might want to do something different.

The teenage Mohini soon faced a serious dilemma: Should she dedicate now, and become a BK, or continue with her education? She said:

My grandfather was very keen on education, and wanted me to finish my studies and graduate. He was particularly anxious for the girls in the family to be educated and self-sufficient, and in this he was far ahead of his time, so I was very lucky. I was educated in an English-medium school, and all my studies were in English. When I asked Brahma Baba, he said the same thing: "You must continue your studies, then decide." Very few of the BK sisters in those days had any formal education, although now, in the late 1950s, it was becoming increasingly possible for women to enter university.

So Mohini went to university to study history and political science, and later earned a journalism diploma. Throughout her years of study though, she felt ever more drawn to the

Brahma Kumaris, and in 1962, the last year of her course, she became convinced that the institution was right for her. From 1963 she started living in centers, for a time still pursuing her journalism career.

In 1974, as the only English-speaking BK sister living in India, she was asked to come to England. She was comfortable with that, she said, and felt she had the right background, as she had been educated according to English standards, and also, while living in the Delhi center, had served a lot of foreign embassies.

But after Dadi Janki came to live in London, Mohini was less needed on a day-to-day basis, although she remained convinced she was destined to serve the West, rather than her native India. In 1975 she went to Canada and, for the first time, also visited the US. There were no BK centers in that part of the world at the time, so she stayed with Indian families who had emigrated to the new world.

Then came a request from the Mount Abu headquarters to go to the Caribbean, where she stayed for three years. The intention was to set up centers and as there were already many Indian people living there—a relic of British colonialism—Mohini did not find this job too difficult. She now recalls that time rather wryly as a "limited good experience":

But in 1977 Dadi Prakashmani, our administrative head, came over and said: "Whatever are you doing in the Caribbean?" implying: whatever are you doing in such a backwater? "America is your country," she said, "you must go there!" The following year, Dadi Janki and Dadi Prakashmani visited New York together, and it was confirmed that I

should set up and run the first New York center. We purchased
a very small property in Queens, and so US service began.

Before long, Mohini was joined by Gayatri. Of Indian origin, as her name suggests, Gayatri is one of the six children of Steve Naraine, a chemical engineer by profession, who later became a minister in the Guyanese parliament, eventually rising to become vice president of the country. Like Mohini, Gayatri had been educated according to English curricula, coming as she did from a British colony.

She and the rest of her family met Jayanti in the 1970s, and were immediately attracted. She recalls:

> *I was nineteen at the time, and on the day Jayanti arrived*
> *a close family friend contacted us to say that a relative had*
> *just died. When we mentioned this to Jayanti, she started*
> *talking about the soul, and we were immediately interested.*
> *I think it was the BK ideas about life and death that*
> *attracted me in the first place. Also, coming from a colonial*
> *background where there were several races trying to coexist*
> *under British rule, I thought that if God exists, he must be of*
> *universal appeal, and not confined to one race or religion.*
>
> *I came from a strange hybrid of cultures because I was*
> *Indian and Hindu by origin, but British by education and*
> *outlook. We had all been brought up according to British*
> *ideas of manners and etiquette, and had a thoroughly*
> *British education.*

Gayatri's type of upbringing—that of a Hindu Indian uneasily adapting to an education and reading matter originally designed for Anglo-Saxon children coming from a northern, Christian country—has been described with painful wit by V.S. Naipaul, in his brilliant early autobiographical novel, *A House for Mr. Biswas*. Here, the hero, Mr. Biswas—an affectionate, though detached, fictional portrayal of Naipaul's own father—is continually torn in two trying to satisfy the endless, irrational demands of his Indian traditional extended family, as well as attempting to be a modern Western professional in Trinidad, a country not particularly suited to either Indian or British culture.

But sometimes this very uneasiness, this sense of having no real roots, produces talent, genius and strength. Although V.S. Naipaul's father was only moderately successful at straddling the two cultures, two of his children, the late Shiva and V.S. (Vidiadar, now knighted for his services to literature) became world famous, world-class writers, offering imaginative insights into a world most of us would never directly experience.

Gayatri, similarly, experienced the peculiar problems of being an intelligent, imaginative child growing up in a colonial atmosphere, where racial tension was rife, and where three distinct racial and cultural types—Indian, black (now known as Afro-Caribbean) and British—were attempting to coexist, and where British culture, manners and behavior were the dominant mode. Of course, all three racial types had been imported into these countries; none were indigenous. But unlike the fictional Biswas family, struggling to hold their heads up both financially and socially, the real-life Naraines were among the elite, educated families in Guyana.

In the era I was growing up [said Gayatri] Guyana was fighting for independence, and there were problems both with the blacks—we were designated as enemies—and with the white rulers. But when the first BK center in Guyana was established in 1976 I saw people from different nationalities coming, and had a wave of realization: If God is truly revealing himself now, he will do so to all races and religions. There can be no racism or enmity between different cultures any more, or any idea that one culture or race is necessarily superior to another.

I had been studying in London, and now began working in administration at the University of Guyana. After four years of this work I started getting bored with my job, and wondered what to do next. At the time, my father was a minister, and he gave me a choice of either travelling or doing a course in diplomacy.

But as it happened, Gayatri's destiny worked out differently. While in the process of wondering what direction to take next, Gayatri went to New York with her sister, and there met Mohini who had just started the New York center. "I helped out for six weeks, then went back to Guyana. But I think I knew in my heart by this time that I wanted to dedicate.

"As my family had all become BKs, there was no problem with dedication, and I finally became a surrendered sister in 1978."

What specifically attracted Gayatri to this life, she says, was not so much the religious aspect as the conviction that here was a group offering a universal message that would touch people's lives and make a significant difference to their outlook.

Even though most people at the time were not aware of a need for spirituality, it seemed to me that they would heed the message in time. I did feel, though, that the BKs were offering a way of life and an outlook that was very much ahead of its era. I also felt that once people became BKs, they were enabled to become successful, independent, confident, productive, in a way they may not have been before.

Certain aspects of our personalities direct us to specific careers, and eventually this seemed the right one for me. My parents were supportive, and so I went to live permanently in the Queens center with Mohini.

Now that the right personnel were firmly in place, the time seemed auspicious to take the next important step: affiliation to the United Nations. The headquarters of the UN are, of course, in New York, only a subway ride away from the Queens center. Affiliation to this organization would, the BKs felt, both increase their credibility and enable them to have a more significant presence on the world stage, working for universal peace and harmony in conjunction with the UN which had been formed in 1945, just after the Second World War, out of the old 1920s League of Nations.

And as the UN was also working for world emancipation of women and a better life for those in developing countries, it seemed the ideal intergovernmental institution for a spiritual movement that had for so many years also been working on these very issues. Brahma Baba, speaking now through the trance medium of Dadi Gulzar, had once or twice mentioned the United Nations as an important and influential institution working for the same eventual aims as the Brahma Kumaris.

Mohini, who already had Indian diplomatic contacts at the UN, started calling them and making appointments to see officials. "The fact that I had a degree in political science made me the right person to do this job," she said. When Mohini first went with Gayatri to the UN headquarters, an official remarked that there were "two angels" waiting in reception, adding that if the person they had come to see missed them, he would miss a very remarkable sight.

Mohini and Gayatri had both adopted the white sari, which was unusual wear for brash, chic New York, and maybe not terribly suitable in winter, when, as the weather forecasts have it, all kinds of precipitation fall from the skies, and the temperatures can be twenty degrees below zero. In those days, saris must have seemed exotic indeed, especially in the ultra-modern, totally Western atmosphere of the United Nations.

The upshot of their meetings with UN officials at the time was that in 1980 the Brahma Kumaris World Spiritual University became affiliated to the UN's Department of Public Information as a Non-Governmental Organization, or NGO. From its inception, the UN has been nothing if not bureaucratic, and the procedure for gaining association with the DPI has always been quite complicated.

Any NGO wishing to become associated with the UN has to send an official letter from its headquarters to the chief of the NGO section, stating the reasons why the organization seeks such an association. The letter should be accompanied by at least six samples of recent information materials, and also, if possible, letters of reference from UN departments, UN programs and specialized agencies, and also from UN information centers and services.

The BKs did all this meticulously, and thus gained their first valuable connection with a respected global organization. In 1982, when the UN connection was well established, Nirwair Singh, the naval officer who had dedicated in 1960, made his first-ever trip to the West. He was on a fact-finding mission to discover how to erect large buildings in the Western fashion, and to discover ways to make Madhuban more "Western" without compromising any of the established Brahma Kumaris lifestyle principles.

He said:

By 1982 we had a significant presence in several Western countries. There was Dadi Janki in the UK, Mohini in the US and Dr. Nirmala in Australia. Westerners were becoming attracted, and it was felt the time was right for major expansion on Mount Abu. Although Brahma Baba had never been to the West, he had been aware during his lifetime that Westerners were very different in many ways from Indians. Westerners, he always said, were sophisticated, critical and demanded high standards.

If we were going to attract influential Westerners to Madhuban, we had to offer them something they could understand and appreciate.

As it was, more people were coming from the West each year to Madhuban and we had no accommodation for them, and only very small halls for conferences and meetings. Clearly, we could not hold large programs for several thousand people unless we could accommodate them.

Our other problem was, of course, that as more Westerners were being attracted, we needed electronic translation facilities which, in the early eighties, we did not have. So I visited Carnegie Hall, and also the Barbican Center in London, to see how it might work. Once I had got some ideas, I came back and we designed the Universal Peace Hall as our first big building ever.

The Peace Hall was built to hold 3,000 people, and had simultaneous translation facilities for about sixteen languages. It was the BKs' first modern building in India, and the first one to which we could confidently invite big-name speakers from the West.

Brahma Baba, speaking now through the trance medium of Dadi Gulzar, gave us specific guidelines for large projects. He said they had to be simple but beautiful, economical to run, time-bound—that is, start and finish on time (which is very unusual for India)—and also be useful. The Universal Peace Hall, otherwise known as Om Shanti Bhavan, was our first building erected with these principles in mind, and it put us in a new league on the world stage.

After a couple of years' affiliation with the UN, the BKs felt they would like to deepen their connection and play a more central role. Therefore they applied to the ECOSOC—Economic and Social Council—for *consultative* status. Consultative status means that NGOs can become accredited as observers to the UN world conferences, and may also gain access to the official documents and official conference sessions. This status also means that an NGO can distribute literature and papers to official UN delegates, making the association a two-way process. This method of participation has been available to NGOs granted such status since the UN's founding.

In 1983 consultative status on the roster of the Economic and Social Council was granted to the BKs, who thus became the first purely spiritual organization from the East ever to be accorded this status. In that year also Didi, Sister Manmohini, died, and her place was taken by Dadi Janki, who became the additional administrative head of the organization.

So from now on, instead of having all the seniors concentrated in Madhuban, there would always be a senior administrative official based in London. Although Dadi Janki remained an indefatigable traveller, her permanent residence was now the UK rather than India.

This was also the year when the first Universal Peace Conference was held in Mount Abu, to which key UN officials were invited to speak. It was not an official UN conference, but by now several leading UN officials had become good friends with the Brahma Kumaris, and they agreed to speak at this conference.

It was the first time that notable international speakers had attended a BK event on Mount Abu, and it heralded a quantum change in BK activities. From now on, the university started to think big, and plan major outreach programs. They were already becoming mainstream and highly respected in India, and now needed to consolidate their position in other countries.

In the early 1980s the President of India, Gyani Zail Singh, had become a close friend, and Indian politicians and High Court judges began to attend Mount Abu events. These were all good signs, considering the relentless opposition the Om Mandali had faced from officialdom in the early days, but there was much more work to be done.

After gaining valuable consultative status with the UN, the BKs decided to rent office space opposite the UN headquarters, so as to have a permanent presence there. Gayatri ran this office, and went to work each day wearing her sari and observing "traffic control" and other BK practices, such as bringing in her own lunch, rather than heading towards the nearest bar or pizza joint, at the UN Plaza in New York.

By this time her father, Steve Naraine, had become Guyanian Ambassador to India, and was living in an ambassadorial residence in Delhi's smartest district. He was thus the first-ever Brahma Kumaris ambassador, and gave many other ambassadors a painless introduction to the BK lifestyle at official functions. The days of seclusion, segregation and dismissal as a "weird Indian cult" were coming to an end.

Most outsiders confess themselves completely bewildered by the jargon, ramifications and committees of the United Nations, and when you enter their vast complex at the UN Plaza in Manhattan your fears are not allayed. The organization seems unknowable, unfathomable, and it is always tempting to dismiss it as "Useless Nonsense," simply from failing to be able to work out exactly what it does all the time.

Unless you are actually working there, the organization and its many offshoots and agencies are totally bewildering. So here follows a vastly simplified guide to one of its most important aspects, the role of the Non-Governmental Organizations.

When the UN first came into existence in 1945, in an attempt to bring nations together to work for peace rather than war, it was understood that governments alone would not be able to do all the work that was required. The importance of working with and through NGOs as an integral part of United Nations Information Activities was recognized when the Department of Public Information was first established in 1946. In Resolution 13, the General Assembly instructed the DPI and its branch offices to:

actively assist and encourage national information services, educational institutions and other governmental and nongovernmental organizations of all kinds interested in spreading information about the United Nations. For this and other purposes, it should operate a fully equipped reference service, brief of supply lecturers, and make available its publications, documentary films, film strips, posters and other exhibits for use by these agencies and organizations.

In 1968 the Economic and Social Council (ECOSOC) stated that an NGO "shall undertake to support the work of the United Nations and to promote knowledge of its principles and activities, in accordance with its own aims and purposes and the nature and scope of its competence and activities."

Organizations eligible for association with the DPI must fulfill the following criteria:

- They must share the ideals of the UN Charter;
- They must operate solely on a nonprofit basis;
- They must have a demonstrated interest in UN issues, and a proven ability to reach large or specialized audiences such as educators, media representatives, policy makers and the business community;

- They must also have the commitment and the means to conduct effective information programs about UN activities by publishing newsletters, bulletins and pamphlets, organizing conferences, seminars and round tables, and enlisting the cooperation of the media.

In 1948 just forty-one NGOs were granted consultative status, which meant that they could advise and work with the UN on matters of joint concern and interest.

According to the official definition, an NGO is "any non-profit voluntary citizens' group which is organized on a local, national or international level." To qualify, such an organization must be task-oriented (i.e., do something, not just exist), be driven by people with a common interest and work for common good. An NGO can provide analysis and expertise, serve as an early warning mechanism and help monitor and implement international agreements. Some NGOs may be organized around specific issues such as human rights, the environment or health. An NGO is not allowed to proselytize any religion, so a religious or spiritual group that wishes to be included must stress its social work and outreach rather than its religious beliefs. A purely spiritual organization with no outreach work would not be eligible as an NGO.

NGOs must also cooperate regularly with the Department of Public Information to disseminate information to their members at grassroots level. The organizations also are expected to publicize UN activities, and to promote UN observances and international years established by the General Assembly to focus world attention on important issues facing humanity.

By 1983 the UN had begun preparations for the International Year of Peace, to be held in 1986, and it was here that the BKs really came into their own. The Peace Hall at Madhuban had been built specially for the purpose of holding major international conferences on aspects of world peace, and now other programs and events were set in motion.

In 1983 Gayatri met Dr. Robin Ludwig, the UN official who was in charge of coordinating events for the upcoming International Year of Peace.

At the time [recalled Robin] it was all extremely vague. We had a secretariat of five or six people, and the General Assembly was mandated. The proposed Year of Peace started with Costa Rica suggesting it and at the time, the US didn't want to know, although at the same time they didn't want to go on record as being against peace.

This was of course the era of the Cold War, and peace was the buzzword for Soviet countries. But as time went on, it became clear that governments were not going to become involved, so we had to go to the people instead. This led to us contacting NGOs all over the world to come up with ideas, any ideas, on promoting interest in establishing world peace.

We decided to take the broadest approach possible, which could be, for instance, conflict resolution in schools, or international festivals celebrating different cultures. We went to major organizations in cities which might be interested, and approached them. We approached Rotarians, civic organizations, women's groups and so on.

We took the current list of NGOs from the Department of Public Information and did a blanket mailing, saying: This

Year of Peace is going to be happening, and would you like to contribute to it in some way? We ended up with 500 NGOs who agreed to do something to promote international peace. The way we put it was to ask a wide variety of organizations to come up with ideas and contributions for peace, which could be anything at all—youth, old age, environmental.

The BKs had always of course been dedicated to promoting peace at the individual level; now came an opportunity to put themselves finally on the world stage by coming up with a global program which would make a genuine world contribution as well as giving the organization a higher, more accessible profile, and make them seem less otherworldly, less interested only in meditation and spirituality.

Everything was now in place. There were representatives of the university in most Western countries; in India they were expanding rapidly, and the idea of working specifically and positively to promote peace rather than, say, simply working for disarmament, attracted them greatly.

Although the Brahma Kumaris had been both preaching and practicing peace since the university's inception, the challenge lay in finding a way to put these concepts across to a world that saw peace between countries in terms of peace processes, summits, treaties and peacekeeping forces.

The major BK precept on peace is that you cannot expect anybody else to be peaceful unless you are first peaceful yourself, and demonstrate this in your daily living. Others are always more impressed by example than by teachings and if you can give a practical demonstration of peace by your own conduct, others will be inspired and know that it is possible.

BKs arrive at peace inside themselves by constant meditation, and by observing peaceful principles in their own conduct. The key to peace, as they see it, is purity within the self, and indeed one of their slogans is: "Purity is the mother of peace."

To be peaceful within oneself means that there is not a mental war raging, but instead a sensation of peace and stillness inside one's own being. The first step on the way to personal peace is to have self-esteem and self-confidence, as whatever you feel inside will be instantly transmitted to others. If you feel negative and angry, then you will appear negative and angry to others. They will pick up your anger and respond accordingly. If you behave in a negative fashion, others will either avoid you or behave negatively back.

Just five minutes of anger between people can bring about a world war, advise the BKs. *Om Shanti*, the greeting of peace by which BKs address each other and the outside world, is the mantra for peace. The words mean, quite literally: I am peaceful, and the more they are repeated, the more powerful they become. Nowadays, now that thousands of books on inner peace, meditation and overcoming negativity have been published, these ideas are relatively familiar to anybody engaged in personal growth.

In 1983, however, they were not widespread, and the standard attitude of most people was: I'd be all right if only everybody else changed. The perception that if we want universal peace we must first start by working to achieve peace within ourselves, was quite a new and startling concept in the early 1980s.

Nancy Falk, an American professor of comparative religion, believes that time spent in meditation enables people to gain the crucial distancing from themselves necessary for experiencing peace and stilling chaotic thoughts and warring emotions. "When you learn to detach, you are enabled to look at your own actions and analyze them," she said.

True peace happens from the inside out, not from the outside in, and it is the responsibility of each one of us, as the BKs see it, to create and transmit peaceful vibrations to those around us.

The BKs believe that peace must be the foundation on which any healthy society is built. Peace must be the prominent characteristic of a civilized society, and the character of a society has to be viewed through the collective consciousness of its members. It is, above all, consciousness that creates the values, systems, customs, traditions and outlook of any society. So, if we want a culture of peace, we must start with individual peace of mind.

Through regular meditation, the BKs believe, individuals are enabled to discover within themselves a vast capacity for peace and calmness. Once there is this "inner disarmament"—which takes constant practice, as with acquiring any worthwhile skill—then peace is reflected in daily behavior, actions and relationships. Gradually then, new, higher standards of behavior are manifested within the individual. The net result is a new social standard.

The BKs believe that the true nature of humans is nonviolent, in contrast to the saying: man is a warlike animal. But many incarnations, much accumulated negative karma have caused us to lose sight of our true nature so that we have lost our peace of mind. With that personal loss comes peacelessness in the world.

The whole basis of sexual, racial, social and religious prejudice is body-consciousness, i.e., seeing others as bodies, rather than as souls. If, instead of saying (or thinking) of somebody as a "black person," we change our perception to "this soul in a black body"; instead of thinking of "a child" we think instead of "a soul in a small body," then classifications based on bodily appearance start to disappear.

These thoughts are the foundation, the BKs teach, for a peaceful world and unless we can learn to separate ourselves from the vices that are causing negative actions and reactions, there can never be peace in the world.

An objection that is often raised in discussion about peace is: surely, if I'm peaceful all the time, this will make me into a doormat, or a wimp. If I remain peaceful, won't this allow others to walk all over me?

The answer is no, not at all, as the practice of meditation will eventually allow you to discriminate, and to know what you want and how to get it. This does not mean you have to ride roughshod over others, but that you hold your vision steady and do not allow it to be deflected by the views and attitudes of others.

Armed with a combination of meditation practice and awareness, the very last thing we are likely to be is a doormat. Also, the BKs can point to their own success in establishing the institution in spite of concerted attempts to have it outlawed. Although they did not respond with violence to the Anti Om Mandali party, neither did they give in to their demands. Instead, the members carried on meditating, carried on meeting, as if the Anti party were not there. They simply did not allow violence to interfere with or affect their work of self-transformation. Would you call Brahma Baba, Mama, Dadi Janki, doormats? Even at the age of twelve or thirteen, some future BKs were finding ways to escape their repressive parents and join the Om Mandali, in spite of repeated torture, kidnapping and imprisonment.

Peace, within and without, had been the foundation of the Om Mandali, and now, with the UN's Year of Peace approaching, the increasingly modern and forward-looking Brahma Kumaris World Spiritual University started to turn their minds towards thinking of an attractive, original and accessible way of transmitting that message to an unspiritual, materialistic and warring world.

They wanted to make a startling contribution to the Year of Peace. But how?

SIX

A MILLION MINUTES
AND BEYOND

It was late 1985. The Madhuban headquarters now circulated queries to all BK branches and centers over the world, inviting suitable ideas and suggestions to mark the International Year of Peace.

What could they do that would be original, lively, capture people's imagination and enable people to think about peace in a new way?

The problem was, as it turned out, neatly solved by three young Australian BKs when they were caught in a traffic jam between Sydney and Canberra in the stifling heat of the austral summer in December 1985. Stuck fast in a line of unmoving cars, they decided to make use of the time by turning their attention to the Year of Peace ahead.

"Why don't we," said one of them, a musician, at last, "ask people all round the world to donate a minute or more of their time to thinking about peace? Then we could collect the thoughts and—"

"We'd soon have a million," said another. "So, what about the Million Minutes of Peace, asking people to donate some of their time, rather than money, as in a conventional appeal?"

"Great! We'll mention it to Madhuban," they decided as finally, the traffic started moving in the tropical weather.

It sounded like a good idea, and it was. The Mount Abu headquarters were immediately enthusiastic, and so plans began to be made without delay. The Million Minutes—yes. It had all the hallmarks of a brilliant idea, being both simple and universal.

By the mid-eighties, people were already beginning to suffer from charity fatigue, from endless appeals from the ever-proliferating charities for their money, and so an appeal that sounded like a request for money but wasn't also had the attraction of novelty. But more than that, if the world was set to thinking seriously about peace, some people might come up with interesting and useful concepts for the future. Never before had the whole world been canvassed to discover what it thought about peace.

The only problem was, the university had no resources for such a big project, either in terms of personnel or money. And clearly, a major undertaking of this nature would need an immense input of both. At this time there were no BK members who had any experience or expertise in initiating worldwide projects. They had already mounted some major conferences at Mount Abu, and some celebrities and dignitaries had visited Madhuban, but the numbers were relatively small, and the conferences only lasted a few days, at most. They were not massive year-long enterprises demanding great organizational ability.

Not only that, but dignitaries were relatively easy to target, being highly visible and well-known. However might one target the whole world? Even though the Spiritual University now had a presence in around forty countries, most centers were small, and had only a handful of members. Even London, the biggest and most active Western center, had only a few dozen dedicated BKs, and their time was fully taken up as it was. Also, few were professionals in any of the areas that would be needed to mount something like the Million Minutes.

In the mid-eighties, the BKs were still numerically a very small-time organization, virtually unknown outside India.

On the plus side, however, one has to remember that the background of the founder, Brahma Baba, was one of business, of selling things, rather than of spirituality. Although since its inception profoundly spiritual, the founding members of the Brahma Kumaris were also intensely practical, and had always found ingenious ways of doing things.

Hadn't the young Dadi Janki received *murlis* through drainpipes and managed to escape when her husband held her virtually a prisoner? Hadn't the Om Mandali successfully outwitted the Anti party, the Sind government and all the irate husbands who demanded conjugal rights from their rebellious wives?

The Om Mandali had been nothing if not audacious and daring, so, surely, organizing a Million Minutes of Peace should not be beyond them? All they had to do was to get the personnel in place, work out the best ways of conducting the campaign, and the rest would follow. Also, the BKs firmly believe that when an idea is right, Baba will enable it to happen—somehow. Their faith in these matters is boundless.

Because the Brahma Kumaris's founder was first and foremost a businessman, the organization has always been more open to new ideas, and far more fluid and outgoing than most Eastern-based spiritual movements, which tended to start with a few followers round a guru. From their earliest days the BKs have thrived on challenges, on doing the impossible, rather than simply preaching the word to a few like-minded followers.

At the time the Million Minutes idea was mooted, Dadi Janki was seventy, and Dadi Prakashmani in her mid-sixties—ages when most elderly ladies want nothing more than to put their feet up and pass their days quietly. Yet the busiest and most productive years of these two founding members were still ahead. The Million Minutes was the first BK campaign aimed at a mass audience, not just those who had expressed interest in BK concepts and teachings, and everybody knew that it needed some very careful planning if it was to succeed.

Although the number of dedicated Western BKs remained small, some young professional people with the right kinds of expertise, energy and contacts to work on such a project were now being attracted to the movement.

In particular, two recent British BKs became extremely enthusiastic about the Million Minutes project. They were Mike George, who had an extensive background in advertising, and Nicholaa Malet de Carteret, a TV researcher and journalist. Both of these had a professional outlook, and were a further indication of how, in BK history, the right people tend to come along at the right time. Mike and Nikki started planning a marketing strategy and contacting people who might be able to lend a hand.

The United Nations connection, which was being strengthened all the time by the work of Gayatri and Mohini at the UN Plaza, had already brought the BKs into contact with some influential and sympathetic Westerners. These included the then Dean of Westminster, Dr. Edward Carpenter, and his unusual wife Lilian. Edward and Lilian had bravely travelled to Madhuban in 1984, not knowing what on earth to expect, and had there fallen in love with the Brahma Kumaris, although practicing and professional Christians themselves. They became convinced that the BKs were a force for good and, when approached, pledged themselves to help the Million Minutes of Peace project in any way they could.

Of course, Edward and Lilian, who were open-minded and wide-ranging in their interests, had many influential and important contacts themselves, and they agreed to get in touch with some of these.

By this time also, the BKs themselves had realized that it was possible for Westerners to be attracted to the ideas and teachings of the Brahma Kumaris without necessarily actually wanting or feeling able to dedicate completely, or adopt the full-scale lifestyle for themselves. These friends of the BKs, who were to become increasingly numerous as the years went by, were to enable the university to undertake many exciting and far-reaching projects that would never have been possible through the work of dedicated members alone.

Now one of these useful friends became involved in the Million Minutes project. He was David (Lord) Ennals, a former Labor politician and cabinet minister, who had come from a poor family and was now a life peer. A former health minister, he had always been interested in peace issues, and was currently chairman of the United Nations Association, UK, and also of the Gandhi Foundation.

He, like the Carpenters, was only too ready to help with the appeal, and arranged for the UK committee to hold its first campaign meeting in April 1986 at the House of Lords. Thus, another first for the BKs took place in one of the most traditional places in the Western world, and BK sisters went in their white saris to the Upper House for this initial brainstorming meeting.

It was felt that the appeal needed, above all, professionally produced promotional literature and also celebrity patrons, to kick-start the project in the right way. Mike George agreed to oversee the promotional literature and began contacting commercial organizations for possible sponsorship. Nikki de Carteret began making lists of possible celebrities who might be interested in lending their names to the appeal, and these were duly contacted.

A rich well-wisher who does not want to be named gave them free use of a smart central London apartment in exclusive St. John's Wood, to be used as the main coordinating office. This apartment gave the campaign a good-sounding address, and made the project sound "monied" and confident.

Lesley Edwards, a primary school teacher and also a BK, agreed to become press officer, and so the appeal got underway. Lesley started work on producing a pack which would be sent out to around 30,000 of Britain's schools.

Because of the nature of the appeal, where nobody was being asked for money, many large business organizations were happy to donate facilities and services to allow posters, flyers and appeal forms to be designed and distributed. Before long, dozens of businesses became involved, all over the world. Four coordinating offices were set up: the one in St. John's Wood, London; one in Nairobi, Kenya; one in Sydney, Australia; and one in New York.

The appeal literature was presented in the style of an Oxfam or Save the Children-type charitable appeal, except that no money was requested. Instead, people were asked to commit themselves to donating so many minutes per day, in just the same way that people are often asked to donate money, or whatever, to a charity.

Three ways were suggested to make a peace contribution: to think positively about peace; to offer a silent meditation; or to offer up a prayer for peace. These three options would, it was felt, attract individuals of any, or no, religion.

Here, as an example, is the Silent Meditation for Peace:

Sitting in a comfortable position, I turn my attention inwards.

I am aware of many thoughts moving through my mind.
The speed of my thoughts begins to slow.

I focus my attention on a star of radiant light within my mind, and I create quiet thoughts of peace.

Slowly my mind becomes like the surface of a lake, completely calm, completely still.

I experience a deep silence as I become aware that I am peace.

And I spread the power of that light, of that peace, across the world.

The appeal stressed that it was not a charity, not a fund-raising event, and was simply asking for contributions of time. It also invited participants to write down on a special form, in thirty words or less, their own personal hope for peace, adding that the best of these would be published in a forthcoming book.

Because it had the United Nations' seal of approval, the Million Minutes campaign sounded—and was—genuine. There was absolutely no catch. It was also extremely original, and this was, as time went on, one of its main attractions.

Posters were designed with the slogan, *Take the World in Your Hand for Just One Minute,* and featured the logo of a pair of hands cupping a globe, above which was a star. The posters were slick, modern, eye-catching, extremely profes-sionally produced. The Million Minutes literature was, in fact, the first that the BKs had ever produced to an exacting Western standard. Previously, it had looked rather third world and Indian.

It was decided to telescope the entire appeal into just one month, between September 16, 1986 and October 16, 1986, and have a grand opening and closing ceremony. Concentrating all events into four weeks would, the commit-tee felt, give the appeal maximum impact and prevent people from getting tired of it.

It seemed that anybody who was asked was only too happy to become a patron, and before long the appeal had collected dozens of names, including that of India's most famous charity worker, Mother Teresa, violinist Yehudi Menuhin, novelist Iris Murdoch, Margaret Thatcher (then Britain's prime minister), politician Rajiv Gandhi, actor Billy Connolly, film stars Ben Kingsley and Deborah Kerr, former Beatle Paul McCartney, musician Dr. Oscar Peterson and actor Kirk Douglas.

At first forty countries expressed interest and planned a packed month of activities for the appeal. But before the month started, no fewer than eighty countries wanted to take part, including some from the Eastern bloc. Very many large companies and business organizations all over the world donated facilities and services, and programs and events soon took shape.

One of the highlights of the UK appeal was the Peace Bus, a specially converted London double-decker bus which travelled all over the country to mark the International Year of Peace. It was adapted by NACRO (National Association for the Care and Resettlement of Offenders) at their workshops in Newcastle and donated free of charge.

As the year progressed, Million Minute events began happening all over the world. Before the month proper started, a number of trail-blazing events were held to spark interest in the campaign. Here are just a few key dates. On July 1 the first national press conference was held in Sydney and Melbourne. In New York on July 15 the UN Secretary-General, Mr. Javier Pérez de Cuellar, gave an official message about the campaign. In Nairobi on July 22 a national press conference was held. On August 14 the British press conference was held at the Savoy Hotel; in Sydney on August 17 there was a major peace conference presenting the Million Minutes.

As September 16 drew near, the mass-selling UK *Daily Mirror* newspaper devoted an editorial to the Australian Million Minutes peace conference.

> *Given the doom and gloom that surrounds us at the moment it's comforting to be able to look forward to something that sounds both nice and constructive.*
>
> *On 16 September one million Australians will be asked to join millions of other people across the world in setting aside one minute each day for a month for peace.*
>
> *The minute can be used for prayer or thought, and the scheme—the dream of a young Sydney violinist—is to be one of the highlights of the International Year of Peace.*
>
> *. . . The* Daily Mirror *thinks it's a great idea, and hopes all readers will join in. A minute's silence once a day isn't too much to ask—particularly for the biggest single issue facing mankind today.*
>
> Peace on Earth and goodwill to all men—*who could ask for more?*

Many other newspapers and journals from around the world wrote similarly positive reports about the Million Minutes appeal. It was one of those ideas that seemed to capture everyone's imagination, and for once there was no carping.

The big day was September 16 and it was arranged that in selected countries hot-air balloons would go up at midday, with celebrities inside. Scottish comedian and actor Billy Connolly, married to Australian actress Pamela Stephenson (who later trained as a psychotherapist), was inside the Australian balloon, and comedian Bill Oddie and the Archbishop's Special Envoy

Terry Waite were inside the British balloon, which went up in Trafalgar Square. (Not long after this, Terry Waite was captured and held hostage for five years in Beirut.)

As the balloons went up, onlookers were requested to observe a minute's silence to think about peace. Since people in all participating countries were asked to observe a minute's silence at twelve noon local time, the minute lasted a full twenty-four hours from its starting point in New Zealand until it reached North America.

The event was exciting enough to be reported in all major newspapers and featured on television news channels, and for the next month a hectic schedule of events took place all over the world. Highlights included a roving peace caravan touring villages in Kenya, and converted double-decker buses touring Holland, France, Hong Kong, Norway, Denmark, Germany, Belgium, Spain and Portugal as well as the UK. There were concerts, dances, art exhibitions, entertainments—something for everybody. Many of these events were reported in the regional and national press of participating countries.

In most countries, both the appeal and its ensuing programs were sanctioned by heads of state or leading dignitaries. The Australian appeal was endorsed by Bob Hawke, then prime minister; in Brazil, by the president; in Kenya by His Excellency Daniel Arap Moi, president; in New Zealand by Prime Minister David Lange; in the Philippines by President Corazon Aquino, and so on.

During the appeal month, far more than a million minutes were collected. In fact, the final figure, computed from the numbers of forms submitted, was 1,231,975,713 minutes, by eighty-eight countries—enough for more than 2,000 years of peace.

The main closing program was held in New York City, in the Cathedral of St. John the Divine on October 22. At this event there was music from Peter Yarrow (of Peter, Paul and Mary); deaf actress Marlee Matlin (star of the hit film *Children of a Lesser God*) spoke in sign language; and many dignitaries from the United Nations attended. Dadi Prakashmani was also there, and the appeal finished with the audience lighting candles and taking them out into the night of New York City. All of those present agreed that it was a magical event, a fitting culmination to an extraordinarily successful and inspired campaign.

Robin Ludwig of the UN said:

> *In a way, the Million Minutes was a test to see how people would respond. It came home to us that on an individual level everyone wants peace. The Million Minutes was unique as it gave people a chance to express their thoughts on peace through music, art and a vision statement. If you appeal to people directly with no hidden agenda they will respond, and I think it made people think about peace in a way they would not have done otherwise.*

The Brahma Kumaris kept an extremely low profile throughout, and their name is found only in tiny print on some of the promotional literature. Very few newspaper reports referred to the Brahma Kumaris as instigators and organizers of the entire appeal, and one can only conclude that their lack of curiosity about the appeal's begetters stemmed from the assumption that this was an official United Nations project. Maureen Goodman, who was also closely involved with the Million Minutes project, said: "We did not put ourselves forward as, although the Million Minutes Appeal was organized by the BKs, it was felt that the project belonged to everybody. We wanted the UN committees set up in various countries to run with the project, rather than ourselves standing out as instigators of it."

In a way it was sad (as it seems to me) that the Brahma Kumaris, who initiated and coordinated the entire Million Minutes Appeal, did not get more public recognition and credit for this. But, according to the laws of karma, or the drama, their day for such recognition had not yet arrived.

After the appeal was finally over, the BKs sat back and took stock. The campaign had been far more successful than anybody could possibly have imagined, and had catapulted the Brahma Kumaris into the big-time. The organization had now demonstrated that it could successfully work with big business, with celebrities and politicians, and that it could organize events interesting and startling enough to command prime-time television slots and picture stories in major newspapers.

It had done all this without ever pushing itself forward, taking any glory or kudos from its success and without any proselytizing, either overt or subliminal. The BKs would no doubt explain all this by saying that Baba had taken a hand.

Anyway, now that the momentum had started, now that the entire world had been alerted and encouraged to think about peace, the public work had to continue. The UN, also fired with the great success of the International Year, wanted its work for peace to carry on. At the end of 1986 it formed a Peace Studies Unit to discuss and draw up future peace projects. As the BKs had, by general consent, put together one of the very best programs of all, the UN unit asked them to come up with more ideas.

"We had expended so much energy on the Million Minutes," said Maureen Goodman, one of the UK organizers, "that we felt we couldn't just let it all die down."

As a result of the great success of the International Year of Peace, the then Secretary-General of the UN, Pérez de Cuellar, designated Peace Messenger organizations which were working to support the work of the UN. The Brahma Kumaris soon became one of the leading Peace Messenger organizations.

"Following the International Year of Peace, the UN decided to award Peace Messenger Initiatives, and out of that developed our next big idea," said Maureen. In 1987 the BKs received no fewer than seven Peace Messenger Awards from the UN—an accolade they could include on their future literature.

The main project that came out of the Million Minutes appeal became known as Global Co-Operation for a Better World, and this was instituted in 1988.

This campaign, which again did not ask for any money, canvassed people for their views on what would make a better world for everybody. Participants could do this either in words or pictures, and the only rule, known as the Golden Rule, was that they had to couch their replies in positive terms, rather than just listing what they didn't like about the current situation.

The Global Co-Operation campaign was mounted with the same intensity as the Million Minutes appeal two years earlier, and all over the world workshops, conferences, seminars, festivals, dramatic productions and exhibitions were organized.

"The sharing of common goals and ideals," said Nikki de

Carteret, one of the main organizers of Global Co-Operation for a Better World, "gave people a sense that their thoughts and actions mattered."

By now the BKs were firmly into the computer age, and the ideas and actions collected from people all over the world were stored in a database known as the Global Co-Operation Bank. These were compiled into a report which was condensed into a one-page statement known as The Peoples' Vision and Principles of Co-Operation. Both of these were incorporated into the Mount Abu Declaration, which included a program of action to articulate a more detailed global vision.

The Brahma Kumaris World Spiritual University had now proved itself a significant presence on the world stage, working for peace, global cooperation and unity. It was businesslike and practical, yet clearly noncommercial, and this was fast becoming one of its main attractions in a world that seemed to be getting ever greedier and more grasping. The simple life that the BKs lived was also attracting respectful attention.

The practice of never asking for fees or contributions was strictly adhered to at all times, and every public event was held free of charge to participants. No fewer than five peace conferences were held in all on Mount Abu, and dignitaries from all over the world came to each one.

Robin Ramsay, the Australian actor who has been a BK for many years, tells a story of when David Ennals first went to Madhuban to speak at one of these conferences. "He was asked what he would like for breakfast," remembered Robin, "and, thinking he would be helpful, replied: 'Oh, just tea and toast, thank you.'"

A simple enough request for a hotel or restaurant to fulfil, but in Madhuban, no such easy matter.

> *Of course, the Madhuban staff were very keen to impress an English lord, and the tea, from a main tea-producing country, was no trouble. But, much as they wanted to please, the Indians at that time didn't understand toast. They had no bread, only chapatties, so somebody had to go down to the village to get some. It was really horrible fake white sliced stuff, all that was available. Then they had no butter. And the only jam they had was carrot jam. Nor did they have any facilities for toasting bread, so they put it on the brazier used for making* poppadums.
>
> *Eventually, after about an hour, a starving Lord Ennals was proudly presented with a couple of slices of completely black, charred bread, no butter, and this terrible carrot jam.*

But these were minor problems, and every year Madhuban discovered more about how to treat Westerners who had been brought up in a very different way from themselves. Many Indians, for instance, actually prefer sharing rooms to sleeping alone, whereas on the whole Westerners do not like to share with strangers. Toilet and shower facilities also remained "native" at Madhuban for many years, and the electricity supply was always uncertain. There was nowhere, for instance, to plug in a hair dryer, and sophisticated female visitors from the West wondered how on Earth they were going to be able to do their hair to look smart and groomed, especially when they were asked to address thousands of people as main speakers.

When one American female speaker asked for a hair dryer, a BK sister looked at her in amazement. "We don't have hair dryers in India," she was told.

But in spite of these drawbacks, many senior UN officials, many celebrities and politicians flocked to Mount Abu for peace conferences towards the end of the 1980s.

Owing to the success of these two large campaigns, the Million Minutes and Global Co-Operation for a Better World, many notable dignitaries, heads of state and celebrities had now heard of, and were favorably impressed by, the Brahma Kumaris. It seemed a vibrant, unusual and completely genuine organization, even if some of its more esoteric beliefs were hard for many Westerners, schooled in a completely different religious tradition, to take.

The fact that the organization appeared to be run entirely by a group of elderly ladies who seemed to spend most of their time meditating was also intriguing, and many Westerners introduced to Madhuban during the 1980s commented on this peculiarity.

But the quality of their outreach work could not be denied, nor could the sincerity and dedication of the surrendered members. Nor could the fact that large organizations such as the UN were proud to be associated with them.

In a paper on the Brahma Kumaris, published in the *Journal of Contemporary Religion*, theologian Frank Whaling of the University of Edinburgh commented:

> *Since 1987 the involvement of the Spiritual University in global issues has further deepened. It has become an effective co-ordinator of major international projects. Already in 1986*

*the university had launched the Million Minutes for Peace
project that reached eighty-eight countries and eventually
gathered, in the form of prayers, meditations and vibrant positive thoughts, a billion minutes of peace around the world. In
April 1988 from the Houses of Parliament in London there
was launched another initiative entitled Global Co-
Operation for a Better World. Again the BKs, as they had
become known, showed their capacity for engaging the co-
operation of all sorts and conditions of persons in a fine cause.*

Everything was going brilliantly. The BKs were now known
and respected in the West, visitors to Madhuban and other
Indian centers were increasing each year, and new centers
were being established rapidly in many countries.

There was just one cloud on the horizon, and that was a
particularly dark one. In 1988 their beloved Dadi Gulzar, the
trance messenger who had been a BK since the age of eight,
when she first had an electrifying vision of Krishna,
developed breast cancer.

It had not been so long since Om Radhe, known as Mama,
had developed the same disease and, for want of expert care,
had died at the age of forty-five. The memory of Mama's early
and sudden death was still painful and everybody could not
help wondering: *was Dadi Gulzar going to go quickly down-
hill in the same way?* It was unthinkable, especially to those
who had watched Mama bravely struggling to cope with an
agonizing disease for which there seemed no effective treatment or pain relief.

Ever since the death of Brahma Baba, in 1969, Dadi Gulzar
had sat in trance, often for eight or nine hours at a time,

hearing and speaking the words of Baba now that he was in his incorporeal form. During January and February each year, known as Baba's season, Dadi would sit motionless and in a hoarse whisper, quite unlike her normal voice, transmit messages and new *murlis* to the assembled throng which, throughout the 1980s, had consisted of ever more amazed Westerners, wondering what on Earth they were witnessing.

BKs were certain that at these times Dadi Gulzar's body was being used, or taken over, in much the same way as Brahma Baba's had during the latter part of his lifetime. Had the effort of this work been too much for her? But then she had always emerged from these marathon sessions as fresh and lively as from a good night's sleep.

But acting as a trance medium was far from her only function. For the rest of the year Gulzar was in charge of the Delhi zone, and also spent much time travelling to other parts of India and to many countries in the West, where she appeared in her real persona: modest, self-effacing yet quietly confident of her role and her value to the organization.

It was unthinkable that they should lose Dadi Gulzar. She must have the best treatment, the best surgeons, before it was too late.

SEVEN

GLOBAL
BUILDINGS

In 1988 Dadi Gulzar had an operation for a radical mastectomy. That and intensive chemotherapy treatment sent the cancer away, and eventually, after a long illness, she recovered. Great attention was paid to her comfort and well-being thereafter, and a special house was subsequently built for her in Delhi, where she had her own staff to look after her.

But the incident had given the Spiritual University an almighty scare. Even if all were Baba's dedicated children, there was no guarantee that they would stay well and be able to continue their work. What would happen if any of them were to fall seriously ill, especially those who spent most of their time in Madhuban?

Nirwair, the stalwart Sikh who had already done so much to modernize Madhuban, to design the Universal Peace Hall, and to make the place more attractive to Westerners, invited Dadi Gulzar's surgeon to Mount Abu in gratitude.

He tells what happened next. "The surgeon said, 'Your institution is doing a wonderful job and many VIPs are coming here for conferences. In fact, more come every year.'" This was true; by the end of the 1980s, literally thousands of Westerners were coming to Madhuban each year, some staying several months.

> *The surgeon continued, asking: "If any of them, or if any of you, come to that, have a serious health problem, what will you do?" That set me thinking. At Madhuban we had no healthcare facilities at all, and the nearest general hospital was several hundred miles away. Also, there were no medical facilities whatever on Mount Abu itself.*
>
> *Dadi's surgeon added that it was our responsibility to provide healthcare, and to have dedicated medical people here on Mount Abu. Nobody else was going to do it, so it was up to us.*

The lack of medical facilities also struck a personal chord with Nirwair who, now fifty, had recently been experiencing serious health problems of his own. These culminated in a heart bypass operation in 1989. As with Dadi Gulzar's treatment, Nirwair's surgery was successful, and he regained full health. But what the surgeon had said was true, and the total lack of medical facilities was a serious problem that had to be addressed.

> *In 1989 [Nirwair continued] shortly after my own operation, I had some visitors here to discuss the idea of building*

our own hospital. At the time we had just $200,000 towards the project, which was nowhere near enough. The Dadis were nervous about the idea as well, as they considered it would be a huge responsibility, and they wondered whether we had the manpower and financial resources to take on something like this. We all knew that we did not want to embark on such a scheme unless we could do it properly.

The idea of building a modern general hospital, able to offer a full range of medical treatment and care, occasioned a huge debate throughout Madhuban. To have a hospital would put the organization in a completely different light, as social work of this practical kind had never been what the university was about, concentrating as it did on world transformation through self-transformation. The Brahma Kumaris had always primarily addressed the soul rather than the body.

On the other hand, one of the biggest problems on Mount Abu for very many years had been that of health. Although Mount Abu is one of the top tourist attractions in India, if people became seriously ill on the mount they tended to die before they could be transferred to a proper hospital.

There was also another factor. Although the Brahma Kumaris had now been on Mount Abu for forty years, they had never reached out to the local villages. Although of course any villagers interested in the teachings would have been welcomed, the BKs tended to be seen by the local population as elitist and distant, rather ivory-tower. Because of this, they were often asked: What are you doing socially? You have these wonderful VIP programs, you do very high-level work with the United Nations in New York, you reach people all over the world, but what about the poor villagers here? What do you do to help them? The truthful answer had to be: well, nothing, really.

Mount Abu has a large tribal population, consisting of a number of remote villages where there is widespread illiteracy, chronic ill health and extreme poverty. Many people in these villages did not have access to even the most basic healthcare, and poor health was the norm rather than the exception. Although the BKs employed a number of villagers for building and menial work, there had never been any outreach to these people in the form of practical help. Now, maybe, the time had come to remedy this.

> *Eventually [said Nirwair] I asked Baba through Dadi Gulzar what we should do, and the answer came back: "Yes, build a hospital. There is now a definite need."*
>
> *We knew that if we did build a special hospital, it would have to offer the best of modern treatment, and be properly equipped. Also, it would have to be staffed with fully qualified doctors, nurses, surgeons, dentists and so on. All this would take huge sums of money, not just to build the hospital, but to maintain it.*

Another problem for the university was that, as part of its remit, it had never asked for money or fees for any of its programs or events. But how was a hospital, properly staffed and equipped, to be run in this fashion? If surgeons and consultants were to be attracted to the area, they could hardly be expected to work for nothing. And there were just not enough suitably qualified BKs to undertake this immense task.

Some more soul-searching and consultation with Baba produced a neat answer, which was this: No, you cannot charge for spiritual work, as this is God's work. But when it comes to physical matters such as healthcare, this is a different matter. For this, you are allowed to raise funds, as the hospital will take not just set-up costs, but also ongoing running costs.

The Dadis finally took a deep breath and said yes, and so the Global Hospital Trust was formed in 1989.

In 1990 the foundations were laid. It was decided to build the hospital, which was situated about ten minutes' drive away from Madhuban, according to the latest environment-friendly construction concepts. The main architect, Sonal Shah, was the daughter of Dr. Ashok Mehta, the first medical director. She had recently graduated and this was her first major assignment. She wanted to create a completely modern hospital that would be in harmony with nature and the mountain surroundings.

The idea also was that the hospital should have a spiritual aspect, and make abundant use of sunlight, trees, panoramic views. There was already in existence a body of research to show that patients recovered more quickly when they could look out on greenery rather than a blank wall, and so all wards were designed to have a view. The eventual design of the hospital was as three interlinked globes, a representation of DNA and RNA molecules linked to form a chromosome. These three globes signified peace, purity and positive health.

So, the Global Hospital was a global hospital in its physical construction, but the concept also tied in with the BKs' early nineties conception of all things global. In fact, during this period, every major event and building was prefixed with the term global.

Nirwair, who himself spent much time traveling around India and many countries in the West to observe the latest trends in medicine, wanted the hospital to be able to offer the very latest in high-tech treatment, yet at the same time give a healing experience of a spiritual kind to patients. The idea was to treat mind, body and soul all at the same time.

So right from the start there was emphasis on daily meditation to reduce stress and inculcate peace of mind. Hospital staff were to assemble for collective meditation in the all-white meditation room before work each day, and also after work. Food was to be strictly vegetarian, and prepared according to BK standards of purity and excellence.

"The idea," said Nirwair, with a smile "was to introduce the Supreme Surgeon whenever possible! But we knew that our spiritual approach had to be backed up by the very latest in medical care and treatment, in order to gain credibility with those providing funds and equipment."

A vastly rich industrial company, the Watumull Brothers, provided the first major contribution which enabled building to start, and it was decided to name the hospital after recently deceased Dada J. Watumull. Thus the name was devised: J. Watumull Memorial Global Hospital and Research Center. It was subtitled: A temple of health and happiness. As well as high-tech medical care, the hospital would offer ayurveda, the traditional Indian herbal medicine, and many complementary treatments such as acupuncture, aromatherapy and magnetotherapy. Thus it would offer the best of the old and the new. Unlike most general hospitals, which nowadays have an element of complementary medicine tacked on to the orthodox treatment, the Global Hospital was designed from the start to be holistic and wide-ranging in its medical approach.

Equipment and supplies could have presented a major problem, but in 1990 a German BK, Joachim Pilz, set up a charitable trust in Germany whereby medical instruments and scientific experiments could be made available to constructions using alternative methods of energy supply in developing countries.

"The idea was to help and promote the Global Hospital," said Joachim, known as Golo, who has himself lived on Mount Abu since 1993, "and many top companies agreed to provide laboratory instruments, anesthesia machines and other equipment.

"We had terrible bureaucratic arguments with the authorities to get the stuff in duty-free, but most of the time we managed it."

On October 24, 1991, the Global Hospital was inaugurated with just eight beds. As more funds came in from well-wishers, industrialists and charitable foundations, the hospital's second and third phases could commence. Although the hospital is a private foundation, its research program is sponsored by the Delhi government. Much treatment is offered free, and those doctors and nurses who are dedicated BKs work without salary.

At the same time as building started on the hospital, a village outreach program, whereby medicines and health-care would be dispensed to outlying villages, was inaugurated. The combined existence of the hospital and the village outreach program enabled the Spiritual University to close the decades-old gap that had existed between themselves and the local population of Abu.

BK Binny, press officer at the hospital, and a local Mount Abu woman, said: "The hospital provided a most powerful bridge between the Brahma Kumaris and villagers. At last, villagers have come close to the organization and feel we are doing something practical to help them have a better life."

While the Global Hospital was being constructed, the London branch of the Spiritual University was experiencing serious accommodation problems. It was now holding daily meditation and classes at the Dudden Hill Lane Community Center, where they had to clear up and make the place "spiritual" each morning after darts matches, boozy parties and suchlike gatherings the night before. They had also long outgrown their London centers which were, basically, barely adapted suburban semi-detached or small terraced houses.

Hundreds of Indians and Westerners were now coming for daily classes, to hear *murlis* and to take the courses and programs, and, on special days, the attendance could be over 1,000. School and church halls in the area were commandeered for big events, and some extremely rich Indian families living in London lent their lavish homes for VIP gatherings. But the need of a large building of their own was now becoming a pressing one.

Space was also needed to house computers, fax machines and office staff as the university's work continued to expand.

There was a further problem, which was that they had nowhere to invite an interested visitor to come and observe the BKs in action, or to discuss future projects. There was nowhere to invite people to lunch, or to hold their increasingly popular positive thinking and self-management leadership courses.

There was, in short, no venue in London that reflected the growing centrality and importance of the Spiritual University. They needed their own university headquarters; but where was such a place to be found?

From the time of the Million Minutes program, their first worldwide event, they had begun to look around for suitable premises. More than twenty existing buildings were examined, but none were suitable for what they wanted. The three senior sisters based in London, Dadi Janki, Sister Jayanti and Sister Sudesh, had a very clear idea of what was required. They needed a place suitable for early morning meditation, and where educational programs, workshops, seminars, lectures and celebrations could be held throughout the day and evening. They wanted a building that would have a spiritual aspect, and that would serve for many years to come, as the university's work grew and as links with the outside community became ever more strongly established.

At last, they found something that was in the right location, and of about the right size. It was a building called, significantly, Globegate House, and was an abandoned, single-story, tin-roofed structure in Pound Lane, NW10. When Dadi Janki saw it, she thought it could be adapted as a meditation hall and for office accommodation. So they made inquiries, and discovered that the site, in a somewhat dismal and characterless, although multiethnic, part of London, was ultimately owned by All Souls' College, Oxford.

At the time initial enquiries were being made Dadi Sheel, one of the original Om Mandali members, was in London. On visiting the site herself, she went into trance to try and discover what should be done. Back came the answer from

Baba: "No, this building will not do, although the site is right. What you must do is to build your own three-story house on this very site."

Dadi Janki's objection, that there was no money for a project of this magnitude, was quickly quelled with the assurance that "the money will come."

A wonderful building could be erected here, but could they acquire the land? They approached the firm of solicitors handling the sale, and were told firmly no, the lease on the building stated that the area could be used for industrial or commercial purposes only, and not as a religious or spiritual building. The asking price for the building was $145,000, which the BKs were prepared to pay. The BKs' own lawyers started negotiating, and tried to find out about a possible change of use but could get no answer.

Months of negotiations dragged on, and came to nothing. Eventually, the BKs approached Dr. Edward Carpenter, an old Oxonian, to see if he could help. Edward agreed, and went straight to the ultimate owners, All Souls' College, where many of his friends lived. He told them: "The Brahma Kumaris are good people who have undertaken many major projects for peace, and you have this completely derelict building. Yet the solicitors will not sell them the lease. Is there anything you can do about it?"

The upshot was that the college not only agreed to sell the BKs the land, they immediately cut the price to $60,000! This was achieved by the college selling the BKs the site rather than the building, and the building was demolished in 1988. As a site only, it was legally possible for the land to have a change of use.

That was the first miracle, but there were more to come. A British firm of architects was approached, and they started work on designing the building. But when the plans were drawn up, the sisters didn't like them. Not at all. The designs seemed to lack inspiration, and weren't at all what they had in mind. What should they do now? Eventually, a decision was reached to abandon the original designs and start again. This time two famous British architects, Thomas Saunders, renowned for designing buildings with a spiritual aspect, and Rod Hackney, a community architect and friend of Prince Charles, agreed to provide designs and ideas without charge.

A BK brother, Ratan Thadani, who had a background both in structural engineering and company finance, agreed to oversee the organization of the building of Global House, and became invaluable in the UK for the development of large structural projects such as this one.

A Nairobi-based company, Laxmanbhai Construction, was hired as the main contractors, and in June 1988 a tree-planting ceremony was held. The first tree was planted by Dr. Edward Carpenter and Lord Ennals, and there was a further turf-cutting ceremony in June 1989.

The design was for a twenty-five-room complex constructed of reinforced concrete. The main auditorium was to seat 500 people and have simultaneous translation facilities for six languages. There was also a seminar room to seat 150, and offices, classrooms, a children's area and underground parking. The reception area was designed to have a permanent exhibition and to be spacious and welcoming.

There was to be a dining room seating up to 100, serviced by an industrial kitchen, meditation rooms, study rooms, a two-bedroom caretaker's flat and suites of offices. The overall design was big, square and imposing, and there was to be a white band round the roof symbolizing the BKs' desire to spread spiritual light and understanding around the world.

It was a very ambitious project, and came at an extremely ambitious price—two million dollars. The BKs at the time had less than one-tenth of that sum. How was it all to be funded, especially when one of the founding precepts of the university was that no fund-raising activities were ever to be held?

Once the final designs were approved, a number of professional BKs living in London agreed to covenant a certain sum from their salary each month to provide ongoing funds. When this had been done, Dadi Janki went to the bank, saying that the university now had a regular income of such-and-such, but the builders needed guarantees that they would be paid on time. As there was a basic monthly income already in place, would the bank give them a loan facility if needed?

The banks agreed, and the facility was set up, even though it went completely against all Dadi Janki's most fundamental financial principles, which came down to the understanding that all monies received should directly benefit the Spiritual University rather than be paid in interest to commercial banks. But here there seemed little choice. The builders would not start work unless they knew for certain that they would be paid on time. But, as it turned out, every time the date drew near when a bank would have to be approached for a loan, the next tranche of money came in, often from outside the UK.

In fact, around 50 percent of the money needed to build the center came from outside the UK, often in very large amounts, from BK members and sympathizers who were in a position to donate significant sums. It seemed like another miracle, as not once during the project's construction did the bank's loan facility have to be used.

The success of this project is a dramatic example of the way that complete faith, allied to practical planning, makes things work magnificently. The secret is, though, never to have wishful thinking, and hope the money may come in, but instead to draw up a bottom line. Once a bottom line is in place, it rarely has to be used. The BK maxim on money is: never hoard, as this dries up the flow of resources, but never be profligate either, as this sends money out and prevents more coming in. Always spend to good purpose, never for aggrandizement, show or ego, and always have the consciousness of donating. Then the most ambitious projects can become a reality.

Not once during the center's construction was time, effort or energy expended on fund-raising appeals.

Once building work commenced, in January 1990, the workers were treated every Thursday morning to the sight of a group of little Indian ladies, some very elderly, in their white saris (and incongruous hard hats) delicately picking their way over the mud and rubble to meditate and to offer the builders *toli* (sweets) while they worked. The topping-out ceremony was held in October 1990 and finally, in September 1991, Global Co-Operation House opened its doors.

At the inauguration ceremony, Lord Ennals gave a glowing tribute to the BKs.

The opening of Global Co-Operation House will be the climax but by no means the end of a great international initiative.

Starting with the Million Minutes of Peace during the UN International Year of Peace, and then the planning of Global Co-Operation as a worldwide project, between us we have been able to involve, through their minds and hearts, millions of people across the globe.

This concept of creating not only a vision of a better world, but an action plan to achieve it, owes everything to the Brahma Kumaris.

It was their inspiration, their organization, their enthusiasm, and indeed their vision that have brought us all together as part of a great international project.

Global Co-Operation House will be the International Center of the Brahma Kumaris, and for all those who work with them.

It will be a source of inspiration to us all.

It has my blessings, and that of all the millions of people whose hearts and minds have been led to peace and co-operation.

While these massive global projects, the hospital and the London headquarters, were in their planning and execution stages, the Brahma Kumaris had not been idle in other ways. Their work for peace, for uniting the world in a global vision, went on. The Global Co-Operation for a Better World project eventually reached 129 countries, and one of the documents it generated was the Mount Abu Declaration, which stated:

What is needed is the spirit of co-operation and goodwill, the attitude of love and respect towards each other, the practice of positive and creative thinking, the application of moral and spiritual values in daily life, as well as action based on a shared vision of a better world.

Now is the time to call on the will and the clear vision of the people.

This declaration was presented at the Houses of Parliament in the UK and at the United Nations in New York and London. Meanwhile, conferences for health professionals, prison workers, educators and other specialized groups were being held in centers all over the world. Sister Jayanti describes how these conferences and seminars came into being:

It all happened organically. We were finding that, whatever background people came from, once they themselves had a positive meditation experience, they started to reach out to members of their own professions, their neighbors, pupils or friends. Our prison work, for instance, began when a woman whose husband was a prison governor came to a meeting. She asked whether we had ever considered doing something for Prisoners' Week.

In 1991 we'd never heard of it. But she worked with us to organize something, and it went on from there. Now we go into prisons, and have many programs for prisoners throughout the world.

Conferences and meetings for healthcare workers began when a number of BKs who were doctors started organizing programs for their peers.

A tradition of honoring the years the UN denoted was

started. In 1992, for instance, Dadi Janki, who had been honored with the title Wisdom Keeper, was a main speaker at the UN-organized Earth Summit held at Rio, Brazil.

Once Global Co-Operation House was up and running, courses, events and programs proliferated. Mike George and Brian Bacon, two BKs with management experience, held courses and classes for business people, managers and office workers, and started producing professional-looking course material.

The university also began inviting leaders from other religious backgrounds to share their beliefs, ideas and hopes, and in 1993 leaders from all the major faiths came to the house to launch the Year of Interreligious Understanding and Co-Operation.

Eminent scientists began attending and speaking at BK-organized programs. During these years, the BKs were nothing if not open-minded and, while never compromising their own principles and precepts, opened their doors to whoever might have something interesting to share, whether or not it accorded with their own vision. The BK attitude has always been: we might have something to learn from these people, rather than: we know it all already.

But although serious and high-minded, the BKs also have a lighter side, and enjoy fun and games. The Christmas pantomime soon became a tradition at Global Co-Operation House, and any excuse to sing, dance, play instruments, act, tell jokes, was eagerly seized upon. When the BKs first arrived in the West, their performing arts programs were, not to put too fine a point on it, dire, am-dram at its worst.

But with the opening of Global Co-Operation House came

a new professionalism to all of their activities, including light entertainment. Actors and performers of the stature of Robin Ramsay, Clarke Peters and John Cleese came to Global Co-Operation House and entertained capacity audiences. Robin Ramsay and his ex-wife Barbara, also a BK, devised a one-man play, *The Accidental Mystic,* based on BK teachings, which went to the Edinburgh Festival and has since played at many commercial venues as well as BK events.

It was exciting to have leading professional entertainers performing (always free of charge) at GCH, but as activities at the house increased, many BKs discovered in themselves talents and abilities they did not previously know they possessed.

When I first met Neville, he was a hesitant, diffident and nervous public speaker. Nowadays, thanks to organizing many BK events, he has become relaxed, witty and confident.

Maureen Goodman confessed that she used to be shy and retiring. Once upon a time, the prospect of speaking in public would have sent her into a dead faint. But now she has no qualms about addressing conferences of thousands of people, introducing celebrities or sharing a stage with world leaders. Instead of being a provincial housewife with four children—the fate she once assigned herself—Maureen has become an accomplished world-class speaker, conference organizer and program innovator. Hundreds, maybe thousands, of other BKs could tell similar stories of how they discovered self-confidence and unexpected abilities and talents through their association with the Spiritual University.

In 1991, the same year that Global Co-Operation House became a reality, the first centers were opened in Moscow and St. Petersburg, and quickly became extremely popular, soon attracting hundreds of students. A large purpose-built center known as the Global Museum was opened in Nairobi, Kenya. This contained an extensive exhibition area, lotus-shaped meditation room and administrative facilities. (Note: what in BK parlance is termed a "museum" is really an art gallery, containing representations in pictures and sculpture of the cycle, gods and goddesses, the kalpa tree and other examples of spiritual art.)

American businessman Rick Alvarez, who became a BK in the early 1980s, has travelled to many countries setting up attractive exhibition centers and museums — another example of an unexpected talent coming to light.

The New York center in Queens, meanwhile, was bursting at the seams. It was basically a residential house, rather shabby, and somewhat uneasily adapted to become a center. Although adequate enough in the early days, it did not any more reflect the work and outreach of the Spiritual University. A "global co-operation house" was needed there, as well. In this case, an intensive search produced just the right building: a former Christian Scientist church in Great Neck, a prosperous, middle-class area of New York.

As the area was around 100 percent Jewish, the Christian Science church there had never thrived and was down to about twenty-five members when the Spiritual University viewed it, but the building was perfect for a BK center. So they bought it, suitably BK'd it, and it became Global Harmony House, serving the same purpose as its similar namesake in northwest London. By this time, the Spiritual University was producing tapes, CDs, books and videos, and so each new building had its bookshop, selling literature and music at cost price.

In America the BKs were not allowed to call themselves a university, as they did not provide accredited courses and diplomas, and there they became known as the Brahma Kumaris World Spiritual Organization. The term "university" could be retained at the United Nations, however, as this word is a literal translation of the Hindu original.

But now in the UK another serious accommodation problem loomed. Global Co-Operation House was great for short, one-day conferences and events, but people were increasingly wanting longer programs, spreading perhaps over a weekend or even a week. Not all of these people had the time or energy to visit Madhuban, where residential conferences had been held for many years. Also, for some Westerners, the idea of going to Madhuban remained strange and exotic and just too alien. What was needed now was somewhere in the UK for VIP guests, delegates and professionals to stay, a countryside place where they could have a deeper, longer-lasting experience of meditation and the BKs' peaceful but productive lifestyle.

By the beginning of the 1990s Westerners were beginning to be attracted by the idea of retreats; peaceful, simple places where they could go to recharge their batteries, take part in programs and events of a spiritual nature, and treat themselves to an experience of peace and tranquillity difficult to obtain in the outside world. Findhorn, in the north of Scotland, had been popular in this way for years (and several BKs have travelled to Findhorn to speak at their programs), and Buddhist and Christian-based residential retreat centers were increasingly attracting world-weary visitors and guests.

What the BKs needed, it was decided, was a retreat center of their own in the UK. So, barely after the final brick was in place at Global Co-Operation House, Dadi Janki ordered an intensive search for somewhere suitable.

Again, they were clear on what they wanted: a peaceful, tranquil place not too far from London which would attract people of the highest caliber from every profession, where residential programs could be held, and where guests could comfortably stay for a few days.

There were, as it happened, some funds left over from the GCH project, and, therefore, some start-up capital was available. Before long, one BK found a rundown place somewhere off the M1 motorway which was not ideal, but Dadi was desperate to get something going, and authorized him to negotiate for it. She was about to go to India, but as it happened, just before she went the builder of GCH telephoned to say he had heard about a place near Oxford which sounded exactly right.

This place was Nuneham Park, a large, eighteenth-century mansion in the village of Nuneham Courtenay, just outside Oxford, and only an hour's drive from London on the A40 road. The BKs inspected it immediately, and realized that it satisfied nine of the ten criteria they had drawn up for an ideal retreat center. Its only drawback was that the main hall was too small. But that problem could, they realized, easily be overcome by putting up a tent in the gardens when required.

The premises were owned by Oxford University, but for several years there had been a serious problem of what to do with the place. Built as a Palladian villa in the 1750s, it had gone through many incarnations since being vacated by its original owners, the aristocratic Harcourt family. During the Second

World War the house had been requisitioned by the Royal Air Force, and in 1948 it was sold to Oxford University. Until 1957 it had been used by the government's Central Interpretation Unit, and in 1968 it became a training college hall of residence. In 1978 the house and gardens were leased to Rothmans, the cigarette company, for use as a conference center.

Rothmans sold the lease for £5 million to a hotel chain which went bankrupt, and by the time the Spiritual University made inquiries the property was in the hands of receivers. The BKs made a bid, and acquired a 120-year lease on the house and gardens, now in a state of some dilapidation, for $90,000 from the hotel company. It was a bargain, although the Spiritual University had to spend a further $400,000 restoring it in the first six months of owning it. There were around forty-five bedrooms, mostly doubles, which could accommodate up to seventy guests comfortably.

The Global Retreat Center was opened with a grand ceremony—held in a huge tent—in the summer of 1993. To mark its opening, the BKs founded a new magazine, *Retreat*, edited by Mike George. Although there were a number of Indian-produced publications in existence, including a monthly newspaper, *Purity*, and a magazine, *World Renewal*, this was the BKs' first professionally produced Western magazine. It was to come out twice a year, and was available by subscription as well as being sold at all English-speaking centers.

The two senior Dadis wrote messages in the launch edition. Dadi Prakashmani made the point that the most successful of all BK enterprises were the meditation retreats "that have enabled souls to experience real peace and empowered them to return to their everyday situations with renewed joy for living." Dadi Janki put in her message that the original idea of "university," which started in Oxford centuries ago, was for people to gather together to experience and share ideas. In the early days, all universities were "spiritual" in that they were religious foundations.

The Brahma Kumaris World Spiritual University, Dadi Janki said, was honored to provide a facility that fulfilled the original concept of the role of a university. As GCH had been a major new departure, so was Nuneham Park, a very English country seat in the heart of the rolling English countryside. Nuneham Park set a precedent, and before long, residential retreat centers in other countries were planned.

The retreat administrator was Manda Patel, and before long my ex-husband Neville left his job as science correspondent of the *Sunday Times* to go and live there permanently. A staff of about eighteen BKs, both brothers and sisters, moved to Oxford to maintain the building and organize programs and retreats. "It was a challenge to all of us to be able to live together," Neville said. "We were doing everything from scratch, including how to live as a community." It was a relatively new idea to have both brothers and sisters living together, and some disciplines, such as men and women eating at separate tables, and sleeping in different parts of the building, are observed. It has long been the practice at BK centers to have *either* brothers or sisters living there, but never both, as proximity increases the dangers of physical attraction and therefore, distraction from the task at hand. Of course, in ashrams, monasteries and nunneries all over the world it has, from the most ancient times, been the practice to segregate the sexes, on the understanding that the presence of the opposite sex can distract attention from spiritual pursuits.

One notable exception to the BKs' rule of not mixing the genders in centers or BK houses was made in Australia in the late 1970s when four BKs, three brothers and one sister, wanted to set up house and run a center together. There was some opposition from both Madhuban and the Australian branch, as all four were young and attractive, but they persisted, and twenty years later lawyer Margaret Newton, twins Michael and Joe Timmins, and Frank Hubbard, who run an export business, continue to live together in perfect celibate harmony, with, as they are eager to point out to everybody, just one current bank account between them.

As more Westerners, with their freer and easier lifestyle and attitudes, and background of casual sexual relationships still rare in India, have joined the Spiritual University, the problems of succumbing to sexual attraction for each other, even when surrendered, increasingly present themselves. It cannot be ruled out completely, and it has happened that in spite of all precautions, BKs have fallen in love with each other and left the movement.

One BK sister living at the Richmond Center met and fell in love with a BK brother. The attraction became overwhelming, and eventually they decided to live together and abandon their BK precepts. She was Indian and he was British, so the relationship crossed the cultural divide as well.

One of the problems, of course, is that BKs are attractive people. BK men tend to be cleaner, better dressed, less egotistical, chattier and altogether more approachable than the average Western man. They also seem to be wise and to hold the secrets of the universe, which can become seductively attractive to women taking the meditation course. My hairdresser, whose ex-partner has become a BK, says that all the women who take the course fall in love with him—but that he has become impervious.

And, although BK women do not pander to vanity or spend time and money on cosmetics, hairdressers or fashionable clothes, there is a purity and directness about them, a lack of guile which modern men find refreshing, and unusual. BKs of both sexes tend to be extremely talkative and lively, much as they worship silence, and, as they smile often, they appear positive, upbeat and optimistic, in contrast to the many sad and depressed people in the world today. When questioned on the apparent paradox of encouraging silence and introspection, and being extremely talkative themselves, the BKs often reply: "Yes, we talk a lot about the power of silence." However, they do frequently have days where complete silence is observed—and I understand this is one of the most difficult of all their disciplines to maintain.

The seniors in Madhuban are very aware that the ingrained habit, or *sanskar*, of succumbing to physical attraction, runs very deep in most people, and the possibility of it happening can never be entirely ruled out, however surrendered and dedicated the members appear. They have a name for sexual attraction: sweet poison. Knowing how all-pervasive it can be, it is the rule at all centers and retreats to be fully dressed at all times when out of your room, never to sunbathe or wear bikinis or shorts, or any provocative or sexy clothing. Visitors and guests who flout this rule can be asked to leave.

So it was an experiment, another big challenge, to have brothers and sisters living under the same roof, but essential, as the jobs necessary to run Oxford needed both genders there. Drivers, gardeners, program organizers, computer experts, cooks, decorators were all needed, so it was a matter of all hands on deck.

The experiment worked well, though, and right from the start the Oxford retreat center was highly successful. Few paid or outside staff, apart from builders and architects of course, have ever been hired to work there. Although no fees or charges are ever made, contributions can be made if wished, and in this way Oxford manages to pay for itself.

In particular, the center has benefited professional groups who come specifically for values-oriented programs, to spend time thinking about what their profession means, and how they can do their jobs more effectively.

But the retreat center is not elitist, and groups of children and youths from poor homes have also come for a meditation and retreat experience. For a large part of the year most of the guests are non-BKs who come to hear about the ideas and concepts for the first time.

There are over fifty acres of parkland at the Global Retreat Center, a deconsecrated church, a boathouse and the River Thames at the bottom. The center is not visible from the main road and is reached by a private road, so it is extremely secluded. There are many delightful walks round about and the whole place has a palpable air of peace and harmony. The BKs have landscaped and cultivated the gardens, and it remains an ideal place to get away from the stresses and strains of everyday life. Visitors have come from all over the world, and it is rare that the retreat center is empty of guests.

THE DIAMOND JUBILEE AND AFTER

The year 1996 was approaching. It would be the year of the university's sixtieth anniversary, or diamond jubilee, and it was time to take stock. The Academy for a Better World, Gyan Sarovar, at Mount Abu, had now been completed, and was attracting high-level professionals both in India and outside. The Global Hospital now had fifty-five beds and many departments, and the village outreach program was well established, taking medicines and basic healthcare to a number of the scattered villages on Mount Abu.

The doctor in charge of village outreach, gynecologist Vinay Laxmi, said: "When the village outreach program was first put forward, there was a lot of opposition from Madhuban. Baba originally said that social work of this kind was not our province, as our work should be purely spiritual,

showing people by example how their lives could be transformed. However, times have changed, and the Spiritual
University has taken on many tasks that were not in the
original plan."

Vinay Laxmi qualified in 1971 and, although Indian, became
a BK when working in a hospital in Edinburgh. She added:

> I was educated in a Catholic convent, and also practiced
> meditation and yoga from an early age, so you could say that
> I was a ready-made BK. I never had any intention of having
> a relationship with anybody, but it was always my dream to
> come back to India one day to work with poor villagers.
>
> I have always been interested in villagers and wanted to
> get to know them. We have sterilization programs here, but
> they are still afraid of producing nine daughters and no sons.
> The village outreach was a completely new departure for the
> BKs, and first began when the Global Hospital was just a
> concept. It had to be proved before it was accepted and as
> with everything else, we had to ask Baba. Nirwair supported
> me right from the start, but of course the hospital itself was
> not initially accepted, either. The way new projects get
> started here is that we always have to ask Baba.
>
> We are actually pioneers in village outreach programs,
> and we liaise with the Indian government. Infections, mal-
> nutrition and illiteracy remain. Many people are anemic,
> especially the women. We are also introducing new concepts
> of hygiene.

The outreach ambulance visits a total of ten villages twice
a week, and antibiotics and other simple medicines are

prescribed. The village women remain very shy and timid, and Vinay Laxmi says they "have no hope."

The outreach program is very expensive and we have to be careful not to fritter money away, but it has brought the BKs credibility on Mount Abu. We have the finances to look after ten villages, but not more.

One day, some Americans came into my office and said: "Meditation is too abstract for us, what are you doing for the poor?" I told them about the outreach program, and said we would like an ambulance. So an ambulance came for us, and that's the way things happen.

The contrast between the smiling, confident, white-clad, shiningly clean BKs and the local village population is dramatic. Villagers on Mount Abu are shy and timid and most of the children are very dirty indeed. The homes are little more than hovels and, in some ways, it seems that the BKs are fighting a losing battle. When the outreach ambulance arrives, everybody clusters round, holding out their hands for medicines and tablets, complaining about stomachache, headache, bleeding, poor eyesight and so on. The arrival of the ambulance is one of the highlights of the week, and when it arrives, all work stops. Men and women stand and sit around, again in complete contrast to the organized and efficient BKs only a few miles away, who never waste a minute.

In India by the mid-1990s there were about half a million dedicated BKs and around 4,000 centers. Administrative Head Dadi Prakashmani had been awarded an honorary doctorate from the Mohanlal Sukhadia University in Udaipur.

She had also received a UN Peace Medal, and was appointed one of the presidents of the Parliament of the World's Religions in Chicago in 1993.

Dadi Janki was given the title of Wisdom Keeper at the 1992 Earth Summit Conference in Rio, and in this capacity also attended the 1996 Habitat II Conference in Istanbul, at which she was a plenary speaker. Both Dadis, now nudging eighty years old, were in constant demand as speakers throughout the world. During the 1990s their schedules became ever busier and although Dadi Janki suffered many debilitating illnesses during these years and was often on the verge of collapse, she miraculously managed to recover each time, in spite of a number of serious operations.

Before Gyan Sarovar became a reality, the Dadis knew nothing about solar power or renewable energy. Yet they were among the first people in India to give the go-ahead to solar and wind-powered generators. The Dadis may never have previously heard of "10 kw of photovoltaic energy capacity" but nevertheless they benignly presided over the installation of a new machine supplying this level of energy. The construction of Gyan Sarovar also necessitated building a proper road, for which planning permission had to be obtained from the Governor of Rajasthan. Building this road generated around 1,000 short-term construction jobs, 60 percent carried out by female labor. New easy road access to the district had the effect of vastly increasing the value of village land, so this was yet another way the Brahma Kumaris were able to help their local community.

By the mid-nineties the Spiritual University had centers in Moscow, Nairobi, Sydney, Oxford and Melbourne, as well as thousands of smaller centers in over seventy countries. There was now an elegant Meditation Center on Fifth Avenue, New York, which had been designed to appeal to business and professional people, and which constituted yet another breakthrough in design and appearance.

Apart from the introductory, or foundation, course, seminars and workshops on self-managing leadership, stress-free living and self-esteem were being held all over the world. Professional people such as Nikki de Carteret, Mike George and Brian Bacon developed positive thinking and management courses for professionals in the West, and these were taken to India, pioneered in that country by the BKs.

Links with the United Nations were being strengthened all the time, and in 1995 the university produced an important book, *Living Values: A Guidebook*. This was dedicated to the UN's fiftieth anniversary and it emphasized the importance of living by universal, core values if we were to bring into being a better world.

The book focusses on twelve higher values. These are: cooperation, freedom, happiness, honesty, humility, love, peace, respect, responsibility, simplicity, tolerance and unity. If each one of us embraces and does our best to live by these values, then the world will automatically become a better place.

We all want freedom, and this word, or a version of it, is incorporated into the charters and constitutions of most countries. Yet what exactly do we mean by freedom? The BK interpretation is that the most important liberation of all is that which frees us from the five vices of lust, anger, attachment, ego and greed. It is from this internal battlefield that all wars and conflicts begin. "The world will not be free from war and injustice" states the *Living Values Guidebook*, "until individuals themselves are set free."

Above all, what the BKs teach is that we always have the freedom to choose our own behavior and our responses to other people's actions. If I am upset by somebody else's behavior, that is my failing, not theirs. Many things, such as the behavior of others, are outside our control, but what we can learn to control are our reactions and attitudes.

It is only by personally embodying all the divine virtues, and becoming a living example to others, that we can exert a positive influence on those around us. And how do we acquire and inculcate these virtues? By regular meditation. This, with practice, say the BKs, enables people to access their inner powers of discrimination and judgment.

Meditation, when practiced daily with proper attention, produces a series of powers. These are: the power to accommodate, the power to discriminate, the power to judge, the power to face, the power to discern, the power to withdraw, and the power to co-operate and tolerate. In other words, the power to remain serene, detached, stable and free of fear, whatever may be happening externally, is accessed through meditation.

"A person who really understands his or her own inherent worth and that of others will come to know that worth is not something that is given by the world but comes from a source that transcends all that is physical," stated the BKs' A World in Transition Statement in 1995. Before any effective change comes about, individuals must have self-worth, self-esteem and dignity.

For more than half a century now, the Spiritual University had been stressing the necessity of transforming the self before positive external change could be wrought: Now, at last, the world was willing to listen to what they had to say. Many books and statements produced for the United Nations at this time stressed this core truth uncompromisingly.

"In the 1980s," said Gayatri Naraine, "we could not have talked openly at the UN about values. But now, this is what everyone wants to hear at summits and conferences. The spiritual dimension is finally being seen as crucial to lasting change."

For many years, the BKs have produced a ballpoint pen, for sale in Madhuban, which reveals a little homily every time it is clicked. These homilies are: Honesty Is Divinity; No Effort No Luck; Be Good Do Good; and Be Simple Be Sample (as they render it). All visitors laugh at the last one, usually putting on a "goodness gracious me" voice when reading it out. But of course what it really means is, Be Simple, Be an *Example*.

In the way they live, the way they conduct themselves, the BKs have always tried to be an example first, before preaching anything to others. Their challenge, right from the start, has always been that of never compromising their core values while taking on board the need to modernize and be aware of new developments in a fast-changing society. "We don't take away," said Dadi Ratan Mohiniji, one of the senior sisters based in Madhuban and an original Om Mandali member, "but we do add on. We have never compromised, but we bear in mind the requirements of people coming now. We have adapted according to modern requirements, but this is addition, not subtraction."

As an organization run by women, the BKs provided a significant presence at the UN's Fourth World Conference on

Women, in Beijing in September 1995. At this conference Dadi Janki, a main speaker, reminded delegates that spirituality was the key to freedom and self-respect and that there were three key aspects to effective leadership: strength of vision, strength of example and strength of self-respect.

In ancient times women were respected for their spiritual attributes, she added, but in modern days these had been forgotten as women became dependent and disempowered. "Spiritual awakening," said Dadi, "allows the skills and qualities latent within to emerge. As these inner qualities awaken, there is courage and confidence in the self and one is better able to face all obstacles and situations."

Dadi also reminded delegates at this conference of the importance of having regard for all human beings, and working in co-operation with, rather than against, our male counterparts, as this was the only way to create a world where justice and harmony prevailed. In this, she was unlike many very radical feminists who want to exclude men. Brothers have always been very welcome in the Spiritual University, but the uniqueness of the organization has been that it is women who must be in the leadership roles.

In India the Spiritual University had become highly respected and parents were proud if their daughters or sons wanted to dedicate, in marked contrast to the days when doors were slammed in the faces of the young BKs, and their pamphlets angrily torn up and stamped underfoot. Since the early 1980s a number of girls' hostels have been established, where teenage girls can live and imbibe BK values, attending local schools in term-time. These girls live in ways very different from average modern teenagers: jeans, pop-star posters and cosmetics are not allowed, and instead of listening to loud music, they meditate.

Not all these girls become dedicated BKs, but at least their teenage years contain purity and purpose, giving them a taste of a different kind of life, if they so choose. There are no similar boys' hostels, though, or any plans for any. As the matron of one girls' hostel said: "Boys are too mischievous. We're not sure we could handle them."

So, much had been achieved. And now it was time to turn attention to the upcoming diamond jubilee, which needed to be marked in India by something simple, universal and special. What better, then, than a commemorative postage stamp featuring Brahma Baba, the founder?

Squadron-Leader Ashok Gaba, a BK since the early 1970s, now retired, takes up the story:

> From the time I became a BK I knew that the institution would expand, but I don't think any of us envisaged how quickly it would happen during the 1990s.
>
> Somebody came up with the idea of issuing a postage stamp to mark the jubilee, and about a year before, we started approaching the Indian government about it. It is extremely difficult to get a commemorative stamp issued, as there are two dozen members of the board, and you have to convince each one. The board looked carefully at all the services we had rendered over the years, and what finally convinced them was our strong affiliation with the United Nations.
>
> The President of India inaugurated the one-rupee stamp at the Presidential House in Delhi and it became a good sign of our credibility, especially as the one-rupee stamp is a

denomination very frequently used. It featured the head of Brahma Baba, and gave us a higher profile than before. It meant that we were now well and truly on the map as an important institution in India.

Ashok, whose wife Brijrani has lived since 1980 in London, believes the other two important BK milestones in India of the 1990s were the Global Hospital and Gyan Sarovar: two projects which showed the BKs to be at the very forefront of environment-friendly technology.

After being at the same level for fourteen years, the university felt it was time to strengthen its affiliation to the United Nations still further, and to apply for general status. This, the most prestigious link, is confined to large, international NGOs whose area of work covers most of the issues on the ECOSOC's agenda. Once general status is granted, the NGO acquires both rights and responsibilities.

Gayatri Naraine said: "It's very tough to get this status, and we had to prepare a careful document setting out our aims, personnel and membership. We had to show that we were truly international, and that our work touched all current issues of concern, including those of pollution and the environment."

A comprehensive document was prepared with the help of lawyer Chris Drake, was presented to the UN, and the outcome was that general consultative status was awarded in early 1998.

I visited the huge UN complex in New York to talk to key officials there, and met them in their small, untidy offices overflowing with paperwork.

Hanifa Mezoui, chief of the NGO Section in the ECOSOC, commented: "There are now 1,603 NGOs in consultative status and they have to report to us every four years. NGOs are not part of the UN, but work as partners."

Gautam Mukhopadhaya, a counselor at the Permanent Mission of India to the UN, was a member of the ECOSOC committee at the time the BKs applied for a reclassification of their UN status. Gautam's office is piled high with stalagmites of papers, some four or five feet high. Peering over these tottering towers of reports and files, Gautam explained how the process works. "With religious-based organizations," he said, "there is a serious problem if the religion is trying to propagate itself. But if the religion is the basis of wider issues, and works on matters relevant to ECOSOC, then we can consider the application.

"Until 1985 most NGOs were Western. Now, ever more are coming from developing countries."

Dr. Wally N'Dow, Special Advisor to the Administrator of the UN Development Program, and Secretary-General of the Habitat conference, said:

> *Traditionally, a lot of the mandate of the UN has been a search for world peace and human welfare. Both of these mandates have historically been the terrain of governments, but today these issues have become so complex and the challenges so great that it is imperative the UN reaches out and obtains intellectual contributions in ideas from other sources.*
>
> *The foundation of the UN is no longer adequate to meet all challenges, and it is now recognized that NGOs have a tremendous contribution to make in advocacy of the major*

themes of the UN effort. NGOs bring vitality to UN work in matters of human rights, environment and norm setting. In fact, they help the UN set norms. If we subtracted the NGOs we would now have a catastrophe. They have been a tremendous force for good, and with the UN are now reaching out through major world conferences.

All these conferences are increasing the involvement of the NGOs. No other agency in the world has the impartiality of the UN, and impartiality is critical when discussing world issues. It is not too much of an exaggeration to say that NGOs are now directly affecting the future of the world.

Dr. N'Dow believes that the big shift occurred at the Rio Earth Summit conference of 1992, where the real practice of integrating NGOs with the UN began.

More and more we are feeling their power. The BKs, for instance, are helping us to outline basic issues such as: how do we keep societies from disintegrating? How do we incorporate values into our work for peace? The organization enables us to give a spiritual dimension to our work. Even the World Bank nowadays organizes meetings discussing the spiritual dimension, and this is going to grow.

We all collectively face the peril of not making the twenty-first century, and there has to be another quality to life other than dollars.

In December 1997 the Janki Foundation was launched at the Royal College of Physicians in London with these following aims:

- To establish a holistic and reflective approach to health-care for the twenty-first century.
- To support the work of the Global Hospital and Research Center in Mount Abu.

At this launch around 300 specialists from health, business and government backgrounds came to discuss the differences between the new holistic approach to health and the predominant orthodox medical model. The foundation raises funds for the work of the Global Hospital and also provides an opportunity for key health workers to come together at symposia, seminars and retreats to discuss the place of meditation in maintaining a healthy, stress-free lifestyle, and ways in which people can be encouraged to heal themselves rather than depend on drugs, surgery and other aspects of orthodox healthcare.

As a grateful recipient of orthodox treatment herself, Dadi Janki does not deny that allopathic medicine has a place in healthcare. Modern surgery also enabled Dadi Gulzar and Nirwair to survive serious, life-threatening illnesses. Orthodox medicine has its place, and complementary treatments have their place, as does a positive attitude, and freedom from negative thoughts and behavior. All must be incorporated in modern healthcare.

The Janki Foundation, chaired by Dr. Ray Bhatt, holds working group meetings at the House of Lords in London, and its patron is Lord Norrie. Unfortunately, both Dr. Edward Carpenter and Lord Ennals died before they could witness this new development by an organization they had come to know and love over so many years.

Never an ivory-tower organization, the Spiritual University's teachers are now in greater demand than ever as visitors and lecturers in schools, prisons, hospitals, drug clinics and local businesses to give talks and seminars on meditation, personal development and new ways of working together in the community. They are active in interfaith organizations, and work closely with those of all religious beliefs and persuasions. They work with healthcare professionals to raise awareness of the value of spiritual health. They work both with scientists and artists, and organize Spirituality in the Arts conferences worldwide.

A new and growing aspect of their outreach is working with youth, especially as young people find it ever harder to discover a sense of purpose and identity in today's insecure world. BKs work with families, and are cooperating with the UN particularly in its efforts for equality of the girl-child worldwide.

The Spiritual University has both a highly practical side and also an intensely spiritual, esoteric aspect. One major difference between the BKs and many other religions or spiritual movements is that everything is available to all; there is no priestly caste, no hidden body of knowledge reserved for the "enlightened" or "realized" beings. There is no inner sanctum. Therefore, although there are seniors and juniors, a unique aspect of the Spiritual University is that there are no leaders. It is open to everybody to become a leader.

For this reason, there are no gurus. The senior Dadis are respected because they have been in the organization a long time, and because they have dedicated their lives to it. Also, they have many personal qualities, such as courage and stability, that inspire respect. But the emphasis is on true equality for all, as all members are encouraged to have equal connection with God personally, and not through the offices of a guru.

The esoteric aspect can be witnessed by all who attend what are known as BapDada's programs: events where a trance messenger, usually Dadi Gulzar, reveals a new *murli*. BapDada is considered to be the combined form of Shiva Baba, the Supreme Soul, and Brahma Baba after he became *karmateet*, or attained a state of perfection. This concept has an echo in Christian doctrine, where Jesus is understood to sit "on the right hand" of God after the Ascension. Such elevated souls do not take human form again — at least, not until the next time round.

These unusual events happen only at certain times of the year, and they always take place at the university's headquarters. Until 1997 they were held in Madhuban but now as many as 15,000 people congregate at Shantivan, the huge auditorium at Taleti, to "meet Baba."

Whether or not you believe God genuinely comes on those occasions depends on your faith, knowledge and experience, but there is no denying the magic of these evenings. I was a visitor at such an evening in November 1998 at Shantivan where a congregation of about 7,000 people, all wearing crisp, clean white, sat in complete silence as events unfolded.

When everybody was seated, Dadi Gulzar entered and sat on a huge pile of white cushions and pillows. Then technicians fiddled with microphones and monitors, and her face was multiplied on banks of TV monitors around the vast hall.

After about half an hour's meditation, Dadi Gulzar went into trance and began to transmit the *murli*, speaking in a hoarse whisper. Its main message was to remind the assembled throng that we are all, even dedicated BKs, at risk of forming bondages and attachments. The strings may be thin and subtle, but nevertheless there is a danger for everybody in being bound rather than liberated. We were also reminded that we should stay happy, not be happy one moment and unhappy another. We should all receive the "special treasure" of happiness.

When the *murli* had finished, various groups of people were asked to stand up and make themselves known to everybody, and eventually, a number went up on stage to "meet Baba." I was one of these. *Toli* in the form of little sweet orange balls in polythene packets were distributed to everybody, and the evening finally ended at around ten forty-five.

At the most basic level, it was a remarkable feat of organization, but what to make of it all? In some ways, there were aspects in common with a Billy Graham rally or other Indian spiritual gathering at, say, the Albert Hall in London. But there are significant points of difference. One is that nobody is asked to come and "witness" on stage, as the people present have already surrendered, and are not being asked to do so at a seductive, mesmeric gathering. So it's absolutely not a recruitment drive, in contrast to most other meetings of this nature. The event is not advertised, and no outsiders attend. It is seen as an internal gathering, not a public program.

Another significant point of difference is that there is no charismatic person at the front whipping people up to a point of frenzy or religious fervor. Apart from the whispered *murli*— amplified by modern instruments—the entire evening took place in silence. Dadi Gulzar herself was completely quiet and unassuming throughout. There was no singing, no clapping, chanting or other massed sound. Nor were there any visible emotions. Nor was anybody asked for money; no financial contributions were sought or given.

As we all filed out, there was a forest of empty white plastic chairs but no mess underneath as when people leave a concert. Certainly nobody could deny that the event was an impressive example of BKs at their most holy, but was it the voice of God speaking? If it was, who or what is God?

These are questions to which there may never be proven answers. What is not in question is that, by any stretch of the imagination, the organization *works*. And if not from God, from whence comes their strength to do what they do without personal reward, without fund-raising and without specifically recruiting new members?

THE PEACE VILLAGE

The existence of the Peace Village, in Haines Falls, upstate New York, is a dramatic example of how BK magic can work.

For many years, the BKs in America had been looking for a site they could develop as a residential retreat center. Although by 1999 many centers had been established in the US, there were still no facilities for holding residential programs.

The search for suitable residential premises had been going on for many years, but nothing seemed to be quite right. Finally, in January 1999, they found what they were looking for. The premises were in the right place—upstate

New York—of the right size, and were being offered at a price the BKs could contemplate as being affordable.

The site had once been a thriving vacation camp, but had been abandoned for about four years before the BKs discovered it. The 300-acre camp, set in the densely wooded Catskill Mountains and consisting of many wooden buildings of varying sizes, was not, it has to be said, immediately suitable for spiritual use.

Apart from its generally sad, dilapidated condition, there were two large swimming pools, a nightclub, a game room, a shooting range and a large bar, none of which had the remotest spiritual application. Anybody could see that the buildings would need a great deal of skilled and dedicated labor to turn them back into remotely habitable accommodation. It took a powerful feat of imagination on the BKs' part to visualize the premises as a powerful spiritual retreat.

However, they felt it had definite potential to be turned around for their purposes, so in April 1999, they bid for it at auction, having already set themselves an upper price limit. Unfortunately another bidder went higher than their cut-off point and they thought they had lost it.

"Some of the BKs came out of the auction sobbing, as it seemed we had lost it," said Ram Prakash, one of the prime movers in the search for a suitable site.

But as it turned out, the other bidder could not raise the necessary cash, so the site was reoffered to the Brahma Kumaris. This time they got it, paying $2.1 million. Baba at work again, they concluded.

"The price was a real bargain," added Ram Prakash. "The site had cost $9 million in the 1960s to buy and build.

"But nowadays, there's no obvious use for these buildings other than as a retreat center. Nobody could really run it for profit as you would need so many paid staff and attract so many high paying visitors. Then, what would you offer them? Nowadays, Americans want more sophisticated holidays."

Less than two years after the site was purchased, it had been totally transformed. The derelict, ramshackle buildings had been renovated and redecorated to provide accommodation for up to 200 guests. The indoor swimming pool had been covered over and filled in to form a large auditorium; the former nightclub had become a meditation room, the shooting range had been demolished, and the bar had become a reception area.

The huge dining room had been recarpeted and cleaned up and the kitchens adapted for BK use.

By the time I visited Peace Village in November 2001, there were no vacation camp traces remaining at all. In fact, it could have been built initially as a retreat center. Although the buildings are low and wooden and of no architectural merit whatever, unlike the grand seventeenth-century Palladian mansion that houses the Oxford retreat center, the vibrations are as calm and peaceful as in any BK residential center. You would never know, for instance, that the basement had once been a gambling den.

It took a lot of hard work, they say, to transform the base metal of the original premises into the gold of a vibrant, clean, spiritual retreat, but it has happened. Most of the construction work has been done by BKs themselves, rather than outside contractors and this, they believe, is one of the secrets of its rapid makeover.

"Most of the workers were amateurs," says Ram Prakash, "and we learned on the job." As with other BK residential centers, the day-to-day cooking, cleaning, decorating and gardening work are carried out by the BKs living there permanently.

The Peace Village, set in rugged mountain scenery, has now taken its place among the motels, ski resorts and golfing centers in Haines Falls, and a formerly stagnant, unloved and neglected place now vibrates with almost palpable spiritual energy.

NINE

SOME PROFILES

With the BKs, as with any organization, many are called but few are chosen, or, should we say, choose themselves. And of those who do enthusiastically join, many also leave the movement.

In his detailed analysis of the Spiritual University, Dr. Frank Whaling addresses this issue:

> *I have heard Brahma Kumaris muse in bewilderment at how anyone who has been in the movement for a long period can possibly leave it. In fact, there are as many ways of leaving the Brahma Kumaris as there are of joining them. The crux of the matter lies in the quality of faith, not as in the Protestant Christian sense of a Luther or a Karl Barth, but in the sense of that which gives a pattern to life and makes sense of life. I have listened to many spiritual biographies*

that have been as different as they were fascinating, and written into them was a sense of coming home when one came across the Brahma Kumaris, of finding that life now added up to a whole and that one had found one's true self. It is possible to lose this sense of faith as well as to find it, to click out of a sense of well-being as to click into it. Or this sense of faith may not suddenly disappear, it may simply grow or decrease in intensity. . . . The fact remains that, in spite of the numbers who leave and in spite of the strict standards that they maintain, the Brahma Kumaris are growing in numbers and in effectiveness year by year.

The relatively small numbers of dedicated ones, outside India at least, are truly dedicated, and work extra hard to achieve their aims and visions. But they don't mind. As they themselves put it, with their endearing predilection for homilies: "A task without a vision is drudgery."

And their faith that God is with them in their endeavors has enabled them to achieve what most would consider impossible, such as the Million Minutes of Peace, Global Co-Operation House and the wonder of Gyan Sarovar.

Although many are initially attracted to the lifestyle by its purity, simplicity and pursuit of the highest personal ideals, as Dr. Whaling pointed out, very many leave the movement as well. Some BKs fall in love with each other and form relationships. Others just find the lifestyle too hard and austere for them. Others may not have ever been that firmly attached, and discover that the BK path is just not for them. Some get lonely and form relationships out of loneliness. It is not everybody's karma to become a BK.

But what about those who do stay? What is the continuing attraction? Here are some of their stories, their "spiritual biographies," as Dr. Whaling put it.

CHARLIE HOGG runs a BK retreat center in Melbourne, Australia, a magnificent house where many innovative programs are held. The Australian branch is extremely active, and organizes many retreats in Gyan Sarovar for non-Indians.

I had always been a searcher, and was known as Swami at school. After studying architecture at Melbourne for a while I dropped out and travelled overland to London after staying in religious places in India. In London I took a series of odd jobs, and in my spare time wandered around all the mystical and spiritual organizations I could find. At the Spiritualist Association in Belgravia I came across Dadi Janki and Jayanti, and as soon as I saw Dadi I had an intuitive feeling that this was the path for me.

This was the mid-seventies. Immediately, the teachings made sense to me, but by far the biggest thing was meditation. I experienced a quality of love I had not known before, and it was the meditation that kept me coming back. I had a completely genuine experience of being loved. I then managed to rent a little flat opposite Tennyson Road, so that I could be near the sisters.

The fact that it all seemed strange at the time to my friends and family didn't bother me at all. Dr. Nirmala came to Australia in 1975, and I started the Melbourne Center in 1977 — where I have been ever since.

Does the lack of a family, a relationship or a standard kind of career bother him at all?

No, I have never felt the lack of a sexual partner, or a need for one. The reason for this is that I had such a deep relationship with Baba from the start that celibacy was easy. I don't think it would have been possible without, as you need powerful yoga to be able to disconnect from things of this world.

I have seen many BKs who experience profound loneliness, but I have always felt very close to both men and women. I haven't felt the lack of a big career, either, and this came home to me very dramatically when I went to a school reunion and met my classmates from the seventies. All looked around ten years older than me.

Also, my parents have been quite supportive and my father helped financially to start the Melbourne Center. My mother was more resistant for a while, especially when she realized I was not going to marry or have children. But I always felt I had to follow my heart—and it has always been with the BKs.

ROBIN RAMSAY'S experience was very different. He became a successful actor, had two marriages and two divorces, and many relationships before finally dedicating himself to the BKs in his mid-forties.

It all started when I went to an actors' meditation group in Australia. I had been on a search for many years but never liked gurus and hadn't found anything I really liked. Also, all the gurus were male, and that bothered me somewhat as I was interested in the female principle.

In 1984 I went to this meeting, and, well, I couldn't hack it at all. I said to myself: They're real flakes, and this is definitely not for me. *Then Dadi Janki came to Sydney and there was great excitement:* Dadi's coming! *I thought:* What is this group? Who's this Dadi? *I went to the meeting anyway, which was held in a dodgy hotel by the docks, and could not have been less interested.*

But as I was leaving they said: "But you haven't had toli from Dadi!" *Okay, I thought wearily, and went up to Dadi for this sweet. Then I looked into her eyes and I knew:* This was what I had been looking for. *I knelt there holding this toli like a piece of the true cross.*

The next thing that happened was that Robin took the Foundation Course.

I found the concept of cyclical time, and the notion that everything repeats identically, extremely hard to take, but then I thought: Actually, it's probably true. *The fact that I was given exact numbers was important. I found the first few years easiest, and it wasn't a problem giving up wine or sex, even though both had been previously extremely important to me. I'd had a wonderful sex life, but I do agree that celibacy is the basis of everything the BKs teach. If you are having a struggle with it, it can be terrible.*

Robin admits that after an initial honeymoon period he went away for a bit, as he found some of the cultural differences difficult to take on board. But now he's back.

My feeling is that you can't run Western centers on strict Indian lines, and everybody has to process the teachings to fit in with their own culture. This is now happening much more, and not everybody has to wear saris and be uptight all the time.

Over the years I have become less interested in TV and the theater. I've had a good career and now I'm happy to let it take a back seat. And now, after tussling with the ideas for so many years, I can accept the organization—warts and all. The founder was extremely audacious, and the thing I most like is that they never proselytize. Also, the Dadis are very open to new ideas.

Robin's ex-wife Barbara, from whom he was divorced in the 1960s, has also become a BK, as has their daughter Tamasin, a paramedic and black-belt karate champion, who lives full-time in a center. "My other daughter, from my first marriage, has a family, so I haven't missed out on that either," Robin said. As a member of the Kiwi shoe polish family, Robin has a private income and, luckily, no further need to work for money. He now spends a lot of time and effort working for the Global Hospital, and says that the village outreach program costs as much money to run as the entire hospital.

MARTIN DAMO, a huge man of six foot six and also Australian, said:

I found I didn't want a monogamous relationship, a little house in the suburbs, a couple of kids, a dog and mortgage, a car and a restricted, frustrated, limited life. This way, I can have lots of celibate but close women friends and expand my sphere of operation all the time. But in order for the BK lifestyle to work, meditation must be something you actually want to do more than anything else in life.

If it comes hard or feels agonizing to you, you may not need it, and you won't have sufficient motivation or encouragement to continue.

Martin, who works as an electrician, said: "For me, as for most BKs, meditation is the key to the whole thing."

When terrible events happen, how do BKs cope? Can they show others a positive, practical example when it counts? Do the various disciplines, the hours spent in meditation, the deliberate inculcation of positive qualities, actually make a difference to attitude and behavior?

RAM PRAKASH SINGAL, an engineer employed by New York's Port Authority, was working on the sixty-fourth floor of the World Trade Center when the first airplane hit the North Tower on September 11, 2001. In an e-mail sent to Dadi Janki in London on that day, just three hours after his office was hit, Ram Prakash, a project manager for the Port Authority, and also a BK for more than a quarter of a century, wrote:

At approx 8:45 A.M., we heard a big explosion and our building started to shake. In a few moments, the glass and metal from the wall started falling down. We thought at first it was an earthquake but soon came realized that a plane had struck the building. Our tower was hit first and a half an hour later, the other tower was struck by another plane.

We took the stairs down all sixty-four floors and it took us two and a half hours to get out. Five minutes after we exited the entire tower collapsed.

Coming down the stairs, we went through pillars of smoke. We were stopped after going down thirty floors because people from all floors were merging. Many times we had to stop to let people with severe burns be helped down. We were stopped near the thirty-third floor, which was engulfed in smoke, and led in different directions. It was total confusion. We saw many firefighters ascending the stairs and they must have been trapped in the building.

When we were near the twentieth floor, we heard another explosion and the walls, pipes and floor were shaking. Our escape was now becoming very slow and people were suffering from smoke inhalation. To make matters worse, as we neared the bottom, water from broken pipes gushed onto the floor with such force that people were slipping everywhere, in total panic and being badly hurt.

We were then led into a completely dark corridor filled with smoke. Wires were hanging over us. We had to go through calf-high water and pass through fallen debris and pieces of metal. Dust was six to eight inches deep and there was so much smoke we could not see each other. We were told to walk along the walls.

When we came out of the building, we had to pass through rubble to get clear of the complex. There was fire all around, and heavy wind created by the fire was causing debris to fly around. After we came out of the complex we started running. There was a loud bang and the ground was shaking. Then the entire tower collapsed.

Dadi, I want to tell you that during this turmoil, I was not badly affected at all. Somehow the smoke did not bother me. I just kept breathing in the normal way. I managed to encourage the others to keep faith and courage and helped them walk through the rubble. I was becoming aware of my duty and role. It was as if I was sitting next to Baba and observing the scene like a little child. I brought three people with me to the Manhattan Center, five miles away from the Twin Towers, and these people, total strangers to me, were happy to be there in these moments of such distress. They stayed in the center all day.

How was Ram Prakash Singal able to keep so calm? Several months after the event, he said:

Looking back, I am absolutely certain that my BK training enabled me to remain calm while these terrible events were happening. As soon as our tower started to shake, I made the decision to move immediately. I now believe that because I was able to stay calm, my body was able to process what was happening and make all the right survival decisions. I was never in a state of shock. At such moments, you emerge what is latent in you, and for me, it was the biggest challenge of my life to remain positive, especially as there was so much trauma, pain and hysteria going on all around me. I believe I passed this test. But I also believe that if I had not been a BK, such conduct would not have been possible.

For a long time, the BK training was all theoretical, but when I had an opportunity to put it into practice I discovered that it worked. Now I think that if I can do it, anybody can do it, although it does take practice. Many people sought counseling after September 11th, but I can honestly say I never felt any stress. On the other hand, nothing can prepare you for something like this and at such times, your own nature, or what you have inculcated, comes out.

After the event, Ram Prakash Singal was asked to do many media interviews and earned himself the title, Mr. Positive. Ten of his work colleagues, all long-time friends, perished in the attack, and Ram had to call on all his reserves of strength and courage to help his surviving workmates cope with the aftermath.

SISTER RAJ, a chemopharmacist working at the Sloan-Kettering Cancer Center, comments:

The three people Ram met on the street who came to the BK Center in Manhattan were shaking when they arrived. They spent the whole day at the center, saying they had no idea anything like this existed in the city. They felt secure, and were happy and smiling when they left after spending several hours in the meditation room. We feel that the BK center met the needs of a lot of people who were in such distress, as we were able to give them an experience of security and peace. I was at work when the planes hit, and many people started to cry. One technician left in panic, which meant I had to cope on my own. Because of being a BK, my first thought was that people need help. Certainly the BK training gives the strength to cope when something beyond anybody's worst nightmares actually happen.

JUDY RODGERS, a psychologist who uses the Appreciative Inquiry method of helping organizations and systems transform themselves, first came across the BKs in 1996:

I had been a spiritual seeker for a long time, and met a BK, Rita Cleary, in Boston. She later called me to say that a Dottie Jenkins was in town, and I ought to meet her. I wondered who this suburban housewife was, but I drove to the place and of course it was Dadi Janki. I felt she spoke from the heart and I was very moved.

On the second occasion when I met Dadi Janki my heart started pounding as if my ribs were going to break. I wondered whether everybody had such a strong reaction, as it was like a cardiac arrest. My reaction was so memorable and unarguable I signed up immediately for the seven-day course, and found the belief system comforting and natural.

I liked the lack of chanting, the emphasis on not worshipping human beings, the silence rather than prayer, and the intellectual content. At first I wasn't sure about the celibacy, but the beauty of coming to the organization at forty-plus was that I had been married twice, my kids were grown up, and I knew from experience that the relationship thing was difficult.

Also, I'd been through the sex thing in the 1960s, and knew it wasn't really the answer to happiness and fulfilment.

Now I am trying to purify my intellect in order to have conversations with the Supreme. If you are in a bodily relationship, this is too gross for such elevated connection. I could see from observing the senior BKs that their intellects were so refined they were able to access messages denied to me.

Judy now believes that the BK teachings are a lot like the methods favored by Appreciative Inquiry. Both are based on locating a positive core, both work with visualizing a perfect state, and both concentrate on seeing a positive future.

"In many ways," says Judy, "they work together and reinforce each other, so that now my work and spiritual practice have become one and the same."

CHEN is a Chinese woman and she and her colleagues have had serious difficulties with the police in trying to start and run a BK center in Beijing. But they have persisted and now have a government certificate permitting them to teach. Officially in China you are not allowed to mention God in public, or teach about God, so Chen instead talks about the "supreme natural power."

When we met in Gyan Sarovar, she said, "Our center was opened in October 1998 by Dr. Nirmala, and now we have fifty students, mainly of Buddhist background. Whenever I am asked whether I teach about God, I say I teach positive thinking, stress management and time efficiency."

Chen admitted that it took her a long time to understand the teachings, and vegetarianism was particularly difficult to accept as only poor people are supposed to be vegetarian in China and she was a rich woman with her own travel agency. "I learned raja yoga only by my meditation experiences," she said, "and I don't believe in getting up at four. That goes too far, in my mind!"

MATHILDE SERGEANT is Dutch and a nursing tutor at the Global Hospital, the only European staff member there. She is tall and sandy-haired, wears a sari and reminds me very much of those intrepid women explorers of the past such as Lady Mary Wortley Montagu, Mary Kingsley and Lady Hester Stanhope, pioneer travellers who never let the facts that they were female and alone prevent them from taking off to strange, unknown lands and ways of life. Mathilde also has something of the missionary about her.

She has a little car and drives it everywhere, often by herself. Most female BKs in India, in common with most Indian women, will never get behind the steering wheel, but Mathilde likes to explore, to be alone, go on long walks and commune with nature. She became a BK in the early 1990s after her family had grown up, and said: "It's been a total life change for me. I spend most of the year here, and go back to Holland every year to fund-raise and make efforts for the Global Hospital. Then the Dutch government will match the money from its Small Projects Fund, which goes to the Global Hospital."

Mathilde admits she likes hospitals, and also silence and adventure. "Because I always wear a white sari now, I am often asked about the BKs. This doesn't bother me at all as I love talking about them."

Michael Hudson, nicknamed Spike, is a former heroin addict, biker and petty criminal. He took drugs of all description from the age of thirteen, and never expected to live beyond his thirties. He was eventually remanded into custody for shoplifting and similar offenses, committed to feed his heroin habit.

Spike now says that going to prison was the best thing that ever happened to him.

I had lost my last job because of heroin addiction, and had to shoplift and bilk petrol just to survive. The period I spent in prison enabled me to reflect, and as I was approaching my fortieth birthday I wondered whatever I would do with my life.

After prison I ended up in a hostel for the homeless just 200 yards, as it happened, from Global Co-Operation House in London. While in prison I kept going to the prison library and drawing self-improvement books out. Meditation kept leaping out at me, and then I found myself just yards from the Spiritual University which was offering these free courses.

I had no money of my own and no job, so it seemed a godsend to me. I went there, did the Foundation Course and it all seemed so obvious. I had decided ages ago that there must be more to life than taking drugs and being a biker, but I didn't really know what. Now I feel that regret is useless, and I have become a fully fledged BK.

Spike now has a flat nearby, and has given up drinking, drugs and smoking. "I still miss smoking, though," he confessed. His experience of homelessness has led to him having a place on the Board of the National Homeless Alliance, and a seat on the Homeless International organization. He has been to India several times and his hope now is to tie up with the National Street Dwellers' Association in Bombay.

"I just think it's wonderful that I have found this nice big BK family," he said, smiling. When Spike first became a BK he had a long ponytail. But now he has a short haircut and dresses in white, or near-white, like the other BKs, in total contrast to the black leathers he always wore as a biker.

American **LINDA KREUTZMAN,** born in 1954, worked in corporate management for many years. Since the mid-1980s she had been interested in meditation and exploring the deeper meaning of life rather than simply socializing and earning an income.

When we met at the New York Global Harmony House, she said:

I had a friend who was a BK, and she seemed to be so light and happy. As I had a lot of admiration for my friend I went to a class at the Meditation Center in Manhattan. At the time I didn't have anything to do with the BKs, but I decided to take their course.

I then moved to Boston, and gradually got more involved in the center there. I found I liked being in the company of BKs, and also something was happening during meditation. The meditation experience began attracting me ever more and I also found the teachings made sense. I had believed in reincarnation for a long time, and I was able to put aside for the moment the aspects of the teachings that I found difficult. But most of it felt natural and right.

I was able to take some time out of work, and started helping with the Living Values and other programs. The growth of the BKs has been very impressive, and the projects they do are meaningful and important. I've been to the Oxford retreat center several times and feel the BKs are giving an incredible gift to people. They are able to offer a lot at different levels, and you take what is relevant to you.

It's a very individual path and probably not for everybody. I don't find celibacy or the lifestyle a problem, and my friends say they have found a huge positive difference in me.

ERIK LARSON, also American, has a full-time management job in New York, as well as being a fully fledged BK. He lives alone in a smart one-bedroom apartment a few yards away from Global Harmony House in Great Neck, and first heard about the Spiritual University in 1985.

I was listening to a public radio program in Chicago, where I was living at the time, and heard Sister Jayanti speaking. I liked what I heard, and felt that the tone of her voice showed complete sincerity. An address was given at the end of the program, so I sent off to the San Francisco Center for some more information. Then I took the correspondence course as there was not a center near me at the time, and read their litera-ture. As I read, I realized that what they said made sense.

I felt there was something special there. As an engineer, I had always been interested in fixed numbers, and that aspect of the knowledge appealed to me. After about a year, a BK teacher came to my area, so we met for the first time.

Erik found it deeply disturbing to come face to face with a real, live BK.

I had no idea what to expect, and had built up a dream world from doing the correspondence course and practicing meditation on my own. As soon as I met the BK teacher though, I knew I could no longer sit on the fence, but had to deepen my involvement with the movement and dedicate. As I was the only representative in Chicago at the time, I became a representative of the Million Minutes of Peace project there. Then I visited centers in America, met Mohini and Dadi Janki, and later started a center in Chicago. After that I got a job transfer and moved to New York.

I've had my ups and downs, but this path is true for me, even though there are challenges and difficulties. But nothing, I feel, has more value and I have learned to appreciate myself as a soul. Now I have the challenge of being in two worlds, that of work and that of being in gyan. I try now to balance and blend the two.

Erik has been married, has one son, and was divorced many years ago.

And now some comments from people who have attended and been attracted by BK events and programs but who would not call themselves fully paid-up BKs.

SHARON RIOS, an American psychotherapist:

I glimpsed the face of one of the sisters and felt I saw God looking back at me. Now I know that God is real. I came into contact with the BKs in America and they suggested I come to India. I had said to myself that never, whatever happened, would I ever come to India. But here I am.

I have been completely impressed by everything. I had no difficulty with the belief system at all, but I did have a lot of questions about celibacy, finance and the role of women within the organization. I was interested in the answers, and I loved every minute of my stay on Mount Abu.

Sharon, an attractive middle-aged woman who wore gold earrings, a black cardigan and black and gray trouser suit, and had frosted highlights in her hair when we talked at Gyan Sarovar, commented:

> *I don't think that I could actually take the austerity of the lifestyle. Although it probably wouldn't bother me if I never had sex again, it's not something I want to commit myself to at the moment.*
>
> *I love the atmosphere of the place, the simplicity and the comfort. In fact, Gyan Sarovar is almost up to Western standards! Nothing is extraneous, though, and nothing is for show, which makes it so different from other institutions.*

ARNOLD DESSER, a former photojournalist and now a university lecturer, was in Mount Abu with his partner, psychiatrist Sarah Eagger, who has been associated with the BKs for very many years. Arnold commented:

> *I am struggling with the beliefs, although I actually like the austerity. During my eighteen years as a photojournalist I have eaten in the best hotels, the best restaurants, and now I don't enjoy it so much any more.*
>
> *It seems to me there is little or no hidden agenda with these people, and by any stretch of the imagination it is remarkable what they have achieved. Right now, I'm poised somewhere between thinking and feeling.*

MARY McENTEE, a former nun from Ireland, now married to a former Catholic priest:

> *For me, there was a sense of pilgrimage about going to Mount Abu. Because I am used to silence from my years as*

a nun, time spent in silence does not worry me. I come from a country where there is a lot of trouble, and have had a magical experience in Gyan Sarovar. As I have been celibate for most of my life, that also is not strange, although, as Catholics, we are not taught that sex is wrong, but it is just not for those on a spiritual quest. As nuns and priests, we take the attitude that we surrender our sexual natures to God, which is rather different to what the BKs believe.

As we are taught that sex in the right way can be a gift from God, I have a serious problem with this aspect of the teaching.

SEROV IGOR from the Ukraine, on his first visit to Mount Abu, said:

I'm a journalist and director of a big TV company, so you can imagine the skeptical frame of mind I brought with me here. But I must say that I have found the BK teachers to be completely brilliant. They are wonderful teachers, and the model of the Golden Age that the senior women create is amazing. In our country, Indian women are seen as oppressed. I came to Mount Abu thinking I was a clever person, with a Ph.D., a doctor of history, and I am leaving as an uneducated person. I bow to all these women who have created this wonder.

A number of "remarkable women" attended a two-day retreat at Oxford in July 1998. Participants included writer and former public relations executive Lynne Franks; Shakira Caine, designer and Guyanese wife of actor Michael Caine;

interior designer Tessa Kennedy, who caused a mighty media uproar and worldwide search in 1958 when she eloped with artist Dominic Elwes; Erin Pizzey; writer Moyra Bremner, who dressed in vivid emerald-green and peacock-blue saris; oil trader Rohini Patel, sister of Manda; and myself.

There were around thirty participants in all, some from America and Israel, and although we were somewhat wary of each other to begin with, not knowing what the weekend might hold, we all bonded as the weekend progressed in a dramatic display of unity; a unity made possible only by the peaceful yet powerful atmosphere of the Oxford retreat center. Sister Jayanti, one of the speakers, commented: "It is easy for women to connect with each other in a spirit of honesty, knowing that we won't be taken advantage of.

"The future of the world is going to be transformed through women, through honoring the highest and best in women. We must also," she added, "awaken men to their spirituality. In order to become leaders, we have to balance the masculine and feminine qualities in ourselves."

One of the exercises that helped us to bond was one where we went round in a circle, whispering a positive quality we saw shining out in the person opposite us. The words were not always what was expected, but we all agreed that, when courage fails and everything appears to be going wrong in our lives, others may see very positive qualities emanating. It's better to be reminded of these than to keep being reminded of weaknesses, failure and rejection.

There were two Israeli women there, and, since that weekend, I hear that the Israeli centers have taken off very powerfully. BKs have not been so active elsewhere in the Middle

East, especially in Muslim countries, and it was generally agreed on our weekend that no area of the world could be more in need of peaceful vibrations and examples.

When women can support each other in this way—and there is a lot of self-doubt and suffering among even the most outwardly successful women of today—we can go back into the world with renewed strength and a heightened sense of perspective to face the many things that go wrong, and all the injustices and unfairnesses that prevail.

We were asked at the weekend to consider three questions:

1. What is my vision for myself?
2. What steps can I take today to make that vision a reality?
3. What could I do as an individual, or what could we as a group do to take our experiences to other women in the world?

Most of the women at this conference would probably never become dedicated BKs, but the experience touched everybody emotionally, and gave a profound feeling of having had a peaceful and productive time together.

This weekend provided an example of the kind of retreats that are most successful at Oxford, where a selected group of individuals meet to discuss and hammer out, in a mutually supportive setting, matters of personal and wider importance.

In all my years of association with the BKs I have never heard anybody say they dislike them. People leave, usually because they feel they cannot in their own lives maintain the rigorous high standards demanded. For others, the pull of a partner and family is too strong to resist.

One participant at our Remarkable Women retreat, a thirty-nine-year-old singer and comedian, and also a dedicated BK, agonized over whether or not to have a child. She is married, living in a celibate relationship, and her husband accepts the BK lifestyle. But her longing for a child was becoming unbearable, and she was in despair over what to do; knowing that, for a BK, one's only true relationship should be with Baba and yet wanting to fulfil her biological destiny.

There is no easy answer when somebody feels like this, and it has happened that some women have become BKs, felt an intense longing for a family, gone away and had a child, and then come back.

One sister, again a dedicated BK, and a professional single woman, was finding the urge to have a relationship with a work colleague to whom she felt deeply attracted irresistible. She mentioned her dilemma to Jayanti, who replied: "In your position, I would probably do the same."

The BKs would not have made such a comment once. It is an indication of how they are easing up in many ways, yet still making the same lifestyle recommendations. Some people have accused the BKs of lacking empathy for others; so concerned are they with their own path. But, as they emphasize, they are not counselors, they are not therapists and they cannot undertake this role. They can only tell people about Baba's knowledge and teachings, and leave hearers to make up their own minds.

The understanding is that, armed with the theory of the knowledge and the practice of meditation, all traumas, difficulties and dark nights of the soul will eventually disappear. For some, this is the case. Those for whom serious problems remain will very likely find another path for themselves.

TEN

WHY, WHY, WHY?

Most people who come into contact with the Brahma Kumaris have dozens of questions to ask the organization. In fact, the BKs must be one of the most questioned institutions in existence. Luckily, it also has the answers—or most of them!

So here is a handy guide to the most often-asked questions—plus the answers. A number of the topics have already cropped up throughout the book, but here the answers are encapsulated in responses by BKs, and by others who have studied their teachings and lifestyle.

Why is there such insistence on celibacy? Isn't sex natural to all species, including human beings?

Celibacy is seen by the BKs as being both its greatest problem and its greatest strength. The organization was founded on celibacy, and this was originally the main reason for clashes with the authorities.

Historically, spiritual or religious organizations that have embraced celibacy, at least for the priestly caste, have had great strength. The Catholic Church was for centuries the most powerful institution in the Western world, and the fact that priests (officially at least) did not marry or have families enabled them to concentrate totally on their spiritual work.

In ancient Rome, the power of the vestal virgins was considered to stem from their perpetual celibacy, and in Catholicism the Virgin Mary is worshipped because of her unending virginity. In Hinduism there is a long-held belief that sex, for men at least, saps strength and energy. Gandhi, who adopted lifelong celibacy in his mid-thirties, was convinced that this decision enabled him to be single-minded and strong in his fight for Indian independence. Mind you, he already had five children when he took this personal vow. However, it was well within a Hindu tradition.

The Brahma Kumaris is unique in that it recommends celibacy for everybody interested in following a spiritual path and not just the "special" ones, those totally dedicated and living in centers, for whom it is obligatory. The reason for this is that in BK teachings the greatest relationship one has is seen to be that with God, and if one is concentrating on one's own bodily needs, or those of another person, this link can be difficult to sustain.

SISTER JAYANTI: *If I want to experience God, the only way is through awareness of the soul. It is much more difficult to be spiritual while having intimate bodily contact* with another human being. Any physical dependency, as we see it, makes it more difficult to have a strong relationship with God.

We find that for many people who come to our courses, celibacy is the toughest problem they have, and one reason for this is because it diverges so much from current social norms. Sex can easily become an addiction, and society pushes sexual images at us all the time. Because of this, making a conscious choice to be celibate is seen as odd.

But if celibacy was diluted or broken, our organization would be that much less powerful. Many New Age organizations talk about equality but in practice you never see it, and the main reason for this is lack of celibacy. We have true equality between men and women, and we are convinced that celibacy is the secret to this.

JAGDISH CHANDER is uncompromising. He adds: "It seems to me that when a person is under the influence of sexual addiction, he easily becomes grossly body-conscious and his identity is lost under the influence of this powerful vice. The roots of many crimes, such as sexual abuse, sexual violence, murder even, can come from ungovernable sex-lust, and I believe that to be addicted to sex can be the worst form of slavery."

DADI PRAKASHMANI: Success has existed in this organization because of celibacy. We can only put our ideas into practice because of it, and we believe that relationships based on vices can only bring sorrow.

Celibacy makes the heart clean. Anybody can see how much love we have between each other as brothers and sisters, *and because of celibacy there is honesty in the relationships. Where there is lust, there is also often anger.*

As to the question of whether sex is natural, an answer the BKs often give is that animals have no choice but to obey their instincts while we, as humans, have powers of discrimination. Professor **NANCY FALK** adds:

With sex, a lot of psychic energy goes into the relationship, particularly when it's not going well. Some people may be freed by intense physical relationships, but not many. Sex in the contemporary world is an attempt at achieving an intimacy that is not readily available elsewhere. When people feel free to express affection, liking and concern in other ways, the need for physical sex lessens.

In American society many people are extremely lonely, and look to sex to connect them to others.

NIRWAIR commented: "Baba has told us that the best way of sharing love is through *drishti*, or eye contact, where souls may commune with one another."

If a married couple both became BKs, would they be expected to be celibate?

Yes. Problems can, and have arisen, when only one of the partners wants to dedicate themselves to the BK lifestyle. One reason why sex is so problematic is because it is the only addiction that takes two people to satisfy. There is always a danger of using another person as your "substance" when inflamed by sex-lust. Also, it is very much seen as part and parcel of marriage and intimate relationships. Upon marriage, one is traditionally considered to "sign up" for lifelong sex with one's partner, so the recommendation of celibacy for married couples seems strange, and has been viewed as subversive by BK critics.

What do BKs understand by consciousness?

During the 1990s the BKs held a number of conferences bringing together world-class scientists to discuss this very issue. Science traditionally considers that matter is the primary reality in the universe and that mind is a secondary phenomenon emerging from the complexity of brains. In contrast to this, the Spiritual University believes that mind is non-material, but plays a fundamental part in bringing material reality into existence.

Some avant-garde scientists working in the field of quantum physics are now exploring this possibility, in the belief that existence has a purpose and works according to spiritual laws rather than coming about by blind chance. There is, the BKs believe, unity rather than chaos at the heart of things, and that when scientists use ancient methods such as introspection and silence they can free themselves of ego and open certain new doors of understanding. Founding fathers of modern physics such as Bohr and Einstein used these methods.

Consciousness, according to the BKs, resides in the soul, the non-physical entity that is responsible for the life force, rather than in the body.

What exactly do BKs mean by the soul?

The soul is understood as the "driver" of the vehicle, or body. It is nondimensional, nonphysical and is symbolically represented by a dot of light. It cannot be seen by any scientific instrument, although in trance some people have seen the soul as being like a firefly, light darting about. It is seen as possessing three divine attributes: mind, intellect and *sanskars*, or behavioral tendencies. All attributes of the soul attract karma, and the main point of raja yoga meditation is to "clean up" the soul, enable it to be released from bondages and vices, so that the divine attributes can shine out once again.

All living creatures, including animals, possess souls, but it is not possible, say BKs, for the soul of one species to transmigrate into another, as some philosophies have taught.

JAYANTI: "I can think of New York and Bombay just as easily as I can think of past and future. Time and distance are no barriers to thought, yet on the material plane everything is limited by distance and time. The soul is different from this in that there are no physical or material boundaries. In altered states of consciousness, the soul can sometimes be seen."

How can BKs be so certain that Brahma Baba was speaking as the true voice of God, or that the murlis are the revealed word of God?

Most BKs believe that time has proved the truth of this. JAYANTI: "The realization that Baba is the true God has come through years of understanding and knowledge fitting together, and all prophecies coming true.

"We have also found, over the years, that when we listen to Baba and receive instructions, things always come out right— even though we may not be able to see it ourselves at the time."

JAGDISH: *The knowledge that emanates directly from God has certain characteristics, as I see it. The knowledge he gives is not only true about the present, but it also reflects the past and the future. If Baba is the true God, what he tells us should be able to forecast the future, and be able to explain how the reasons of the past become the cause of the future. The knowledge of God has this special feature which is that it tells us today about what will happen in, say, twenty years' time. Over the years I have realized that what Baba tells us has always been coming true. And what he has spoken about the past has also been nothing but true.*

In the beginning, the BKs were giving revelations that were against tradition and what people believed. Second, there has always been emphasis on the very highest qualities: total purity, total honesty, total holiness—with no compromises. In my close contact with Baba over the years I have never found anything but divine attributes. Evil and anger are never condemned or condoned, and even when there was a lot of persecution, we were told never to be unkind in return. We are taught that we are all brother souls, and there was never vengeance or hatred against our persecutors.

I have studied many other religions, and have found such huge gaps that it is impossible to believe what they are alleging. But Baba has always answered everything in ways we can understand.

The *murlis*, say BKs, have a consistency about them which is not found in other "channeled" literature, where inconsistencies are rife.

Who, or what, is God, as the BKs understand him/her?

God is a spiritual being who does not possess any physical form or dimensions. He is eternal and forever unchanging. In fact, his attributes are expressed in the Western hymn:

> *Immortal, invisible, God only wise,*
> *In light, inaccessible, hid from our eyes,*
> *Most blessed, most glorious, the Ancient of Days,*
> *Almighty, victorious, thy great name we praise.*
>
> *Unresting, unhasting and silent as light,*
> *Nor wanting, nor wasting, thou rulest in might,*
> *Thy justice like mountains high soaring above,*
> *Thy clouds which are fountains of goodness and love.*
>
> *To all life Thou givest, to both great and small;*
> *In all life thou livest, the true life of all;*
> *We blossom and flourish, as leaves on the tree,*
> *And wither, and perish — but nought changeth thee.*
>
> *Great Father of Glory, pure Father of Light,*
> *Thine angels adore thee, all veiling their sight;*
> *All laud we would render; O help us to see*
> *'Tis only the splendour of light hideth thee.*

God does not, as the BKs understand it, involve himself in the world of matter except when it is time for the world to renew itself. Then he speaks directly through a prophet or messenger. Abraham, Jesus Christ, Mohammed, were examples of these messengers. God does not cause evil to happen: We cause it ourselves. And it is only by linking ourselves with God that we can learn to distinguish truth from falsehood, good from evil.

There are not "bits" of God in all of us, as some Hindu doctrines believe. The BKs do not adhere to the doctrine of omnipresence. Our individual souls are separate from God and, although divine, are not part of the Supreme.

Would the BKs consider themselves to be a religion?

The BKs are not a religion in the sense that there is no book of scriptures, no dogma, ritual, priests or gurus. There is no Bible in the BK movement, although the *murlis* come close. But they are more like sermons, admonitions and encouragements than actual scriptures. The Spiritual University does not seek to gain converts, but simply wishes to offer an understanding of the spiritual dimension of life for all who wish to hear it.

Sogyal Rinpoche, in his *Tibetan Book of Living and Dying*, has this to say:

> Human beings have come to a critical phase in their evolution, and this age of extreme confusion demands a teaching of comparably extreme power and clarity. I have also found that modern people want a path shorn of dogma, fundamentalism, exclusivity, complex metaphysics and culturally exotic paraphernalia, a path at once simple and profound, a path that does not need to be practised in ashrams or monasteries but one that can be integrated with ordinary life and practiced anywhere.

He is talking about his own spiritual path, that of Tibetan Buddhism, but it also very clearly describes the appeal of the Spiritual University.

What evidence is there for the 5,000 year cycle, which goes against present-day teachings on evolution?

This one is endlessly debated in BK gatherings.

JAGDISH: *In this age, almost everybody is now taught that this world is billions of years old. But when we look at the population growth, how can it come to the present figure, starting with the time of Jewish history? If there had been millions and billions of years, the population would be incalculable by now.*

Also, there is no recorded history beyond around 2,500 years ago. They just call it prehistory, but it is based on nothing but assumption. Plus, how can life come from nonlife?

BRIJ MOHAN, a senior brother and editor of *Purity* newspaper, adds:

The laws of thermodynamics state that nothing can be created or destroyed. Time has never begun and it will never end, as everything in nature is cyclic. Nobody has ever been able to say how things came into existence, but everything is created new in physical terms and becomes old, rather than the other way around. We always ask: which came first, the seed or the tree, the chicken or the egg?

Anything inside the material system is subject to entropy and decay. The sun is not part of this process. As we see it, the theory of evolution runs contrary to the laws of thermodynamics and spirituality. Everybody nowadays is frightened of nonrenewable sources of energy, but nothing in nature is nonrenewable. Seeds, for instance, never die—they only change their form. Once we take on board the idea of cyclic time all fears vanish.

This doctrine, like that of evolution, can probably never be finally proved one way or the other, but it does at least have the appeal of making logical sense. Nobody yet knows exactly how the world will destroy and renew itself, and many theories abound. It is thought by some BKs that dinosaurs and other "prehistoric" animals are mutants from a nuclear holocaust, but there is no proof of this.

Baba has said in some *murlis* that the end of the world, as we know it, will eventually come about through financial problems rather than anything else.

But haven't religions predicted for centuries that the end of the world is nigh? Yet it never happens?

The BKs believe that the end of the world in its present state must come fairly soon, as the vices are so prevalent. But the main difference between their doctrines and those of other doomsday cults is that the world renews itself. It does not come to an end, as such; only in its present form.

If time repeats identically every 5,000 years, why don't we remember any of it?

One simple answer to this is that we don't remember everything that happened yesterday, or last year, never mind what happened 5,000 years ago. But if something repeats identically, it is in the nature of things that we wouldn't remember, because if we remembered, there would be a sense of déjà vu about it, and therefore it would not be identical.

For instance, if we hear a piece of music at three o'clock in the afternoon, and then play that same piece of music at five o'clock, the experience is subtly different the second time round. For one thing, time will have moved on. For another, having heard it once we may not enjoy it so much the second time round, or we may be interrupted. Or there may be a scratch on the disc. In order for the experience to be repeated identically, we would have to go back to three o'clock and start again, from that exact point in time.

When BKs say everything repeats identically, this means it repeats *as if for the first time.* Nevertheless, it has happened before and will happen again. This is a difficult concept to grasp, but explains how some people can foretell the future, or accurately dream the future. If the future were not already "written" this would not be possible, nor would it be possible for some astrologers and psychics to foretell events with accuracy.

If everything repeats identically and everything is fixed within the drama, what's the point in making any effort? If it's going to happen anyway, why don't we just sit back and let it?

Theologians have argued over this without coming to a satisfactory conclusion. The BKs themselves are currently making strenuous efforts to bring about a better world; they would say, that's why we're here. It is part of the drama for us to make effort—especially as we ourselves don't know what's coming, even though it may be "written." In the meantime, we as individuals are happier, more content, more positive, about ourselves, if we make effort and lead purposeful lives, rather than indulging in shallow hedonism.

What is the difference between knowledge and faith?

DADI PRAKASHMANI: "Information is knowledge, but if I have not seen a place I have to have faith that it exists. I may never have been to Paris, but there is so much information about the place that I have to believe it exists. I have to have faith in the information."

Who judges right and wrong?

DADI PRAKASHMANI: *The only way to know the difference between right and wrong is to become soul-conscious. Deep meditation accesses knowledge which gives the basis to judge, and, with practice, you come to have the knowledge that you are doing the best you can. When you are not meditating, judgment is not there.*

If you have the feeling that you belong to everyone, and look after everybody as a trustee, you are enabled to do right actions. By having love rather than attachment you learn discrimination.

How does a soul choose which body to enter? Does a male enter a male again, or what?

BRIJ MOHAN: "It comes about through automatic selection. I don't decide to leave the body but it happens when our allotted timespan in one particular body is over. The personality traits in each individual make the decision, and it's this factor which automatically selects friends, enemies and so on. Selection depends on entitlement and the next body could be male or female."

What is the time span between incarnations?

The BKs believe that, for karmic reasons, rebirth happens almost immediately, and date the entry of a soul into a new body at the time of the "quickening," or at about four months' gestation. Some scientific research is now showing that unborn babies have definite personalities in the womb: Some are quiet and compliant, while others appear adventurous and rebellious; these traits are carried through after birth.

As the BKs don't charge any fees for courses or events, where does all the money come from?

The usual answer given is voluntary contributions. But this doesn't really answer the question of how a complex and successful world organization can fund itself without ever making charges. In every center there are boxes scattered around into which students and participants can put contributions. Monies collected from these boxes tend to keep centers ticking along, but they do not allow for large building programs.

Much of the big money for major expansion in the 1990s has come from wealthy individuals who feel they want to use their money for good work, and can't imagine any better cause than the BKs. Sometimes, very large contributions are offered in this way. Money also comes from inheritances, and people leaving the BKs money in their wills.

Many BK professionals, manufacturers and suppliers donate time, expertise, foodstuffs or computer equipment. One Indian BK, for instance, who owns a large cotton mill, supplies T-shirts and underwear free of charge. Of course, no salaries are paid and every BK lives a no-frills lifestyle, so this cuts down costs.

If somebody wants to become a dedicated BK, their finances are very carefully assessed, as the Dadis do not want people to be a drain on the parish; nor do they want to spend time and effort dishing out small sums for fares, toiletries and so on. A prospective surrendered BK must either have a sponsor or some funds of their own. In India it is often the case that dowries are given to the organization. In the West BKs are encouraged to have a part-time job, at least, unless they have access to continuing funds.

Some BKs use inheritances or money from the sale of a house, for instance, to fund their BK lifestyle.

Every case is taken on its own merits, and careful steps are taken to ensure that the solution suits all parties involved. Very often, when people newly dedicate, they are keen to give all their worldly wealth to the organization. But the BKs will look at the situation carefully, and in the long term, knowing that such enthusiasm does not always last, and that there may be dependents in the family.

BKs in full-time work are expected to donate a proportion of their income to the Spiritual University. But, always, their family or dependents must come first. Only after they can feed and clothe themselves and their dependents, will the Dadis accept sizeable contributions.

Why do women have to be in charge?

It is laid down in the constitution that the Spiritual University must always be headed by a female, although this does not have to be an Indian woman. A Western woman, if suitable, could become the head. At one level, this insistence is an attempt to redress the imbalance of centuries, where women have never been allowed to be spiritual leaders, only followers.

But there are other, more spiritual reasons. One is that women tend to have less ego than men and are less likely to want to divide and rule. Another is that women are the mothers, and so looking after a family comes more naturally to them.

> **DADI PRAKASHMANI:** *The qualities of women are love and renunciation, nurturing and tolerance. There are the feelings of serving others. In nature, the sun gives light and, together with light, gives heat. The heat of the sun is endlessly tolerated by Mother Earth. Who tolerates? Not the sun, but Mother Earth.*
>
> *Again, from the ocean water brings rain. Too much rain equals floods. Again, who tolerates? Mother Earth. The sun may help but it doesn't tolerate. There are so many examples of why the Earth is compared to a mother. A mother's love attracts people, and the mother gives contribution but does not expect anything in return.*

Another point made by one of the Dadis is that women make better teachers, and the sisters keep everyone together. Many organizations disintegrate after the guru has gone, but Baba trained the sisters in such a way that they learned how to keep everybody part of the community.

The BK lifestyle seems very bleak to most of us. Why do they have to get up at 4:00 A.M., for instance?

The BK lifestyle is certainly not intended as bleak! Much bliss and power is experienced in early morning meditation, and the lifestyle and diet are intended to make people happy, not miserable, as it is all part of the process of separating oneself from vices and negativity. As the emphasis is on inculcating spiritual, rather than physical, values, the BKs do not seek any kind of ostentation. Their lives are simple, but intended to promote physical, mental and emotional health.

For instance, many people become ill when visiting India. But because of the pure food the BKs serve, incidences of illness are far less in BK centers than other parts of India. The more one embarks on a BK lifestyle, the more gross and unnecessary many physical pleasures seem to become.

The BKs do not allow smoking, drinking alcohol, meat eating or sexual activity in any of their centers and retreats. The purpose of this is not to spoil anybody's fun but to maximize the spiritual, peaceful atmosphere of the place.

Are all centers run in exactly the same way, or are allowances made for different countries, different cultures?

Although all centers follow the same basic principles, there is definitely a noticeable national flavor. The French centers tend to be extremely chic, the German ones functional, the Australian ones laid-back and the British ones rather formal. In the early days a strict Indian model was laid down for foreign centers, but now there is far more flexibility. Early Western female BKs, for instance, were expected to wear a white sari and have their hair in a long pigtail down their backs. But now, Western clothes and hairstyles are common in Western centers.

What are the main points of the teachings as given in the Foundation Course?

This course takes place over seven days, and has been refined considerably over the years. The first lesson emphasizes the importance of the soul, which has three separate, interlinked qualities: the mind, intellect and behavioral tendencies, or *sanskars.*

The second lesson explains the nature of God the Supreme, and the three worlds of existence. The first is the physical world of matter and physical elements; the second is the world of light known as the subtle region; and the third is the incorporeal or supreme world, the home of stability, silence and peace. This is the world from which all souls come and which can be reached through intense meditation.

The third lesson explains how raja yoga meditation can help us access the soul world.

The fourth lesson explains the nature of karma, or the law of cause and effect. According to these laws, all actions have consequences, which can be either good or bad and which will rebound in like kind upon the perpetrator. Closely allied to the law of karma is the idea of reincarnation, and BKs believe that we take a succession of births according to actions carried out in previous incarnations.

It seems to us that the world is full of injustice and unfairness. In fact, say the BKs, this is karma working itself out. When we understand karma, we can be more responsible about our own actions, in the understanding that nothing goes unnoticed.

The fifth lesson concentrates on the cycle, and an explanation of the Gold, Silver, Copper, Iron and Confluence Ages. There are around a million souls in existence at the beginning of each cycle, and this number gradually increases as more souls descend throughout the ages, or *kalpa*. At the end of the Iron Age, God directly intervenes to bring his children back to goodness and love.

The sixth lesson explains how Brahma Baba fits into all this, as BKs believe that God descended into his body in order to benefit humanity. Brahma Baba has now joined with God in this subtle region, and the understanding is that Mama is now in another body.

The seventh lesson gives a quick guide to the eternal, or *kalpa* tree, and outlines the part played by religions and civilizations through the various ages. The Spiritual University holds the world's great religions, such as Hinduism, Judaism, Buddhism, Christianity and Islam, in high esteem, although believing that ultimately they have been unable to stem the tide of human depravity.

What are the secrets of the BKs' success?

There are many answers to this question, so I will just give a selection of the best:

> **JAYANTI:** *People like us because we are genuinely noncommercial and there is no hidden catch. Also, there are no gurus, and having a guru spells influence, blind faith and misdeeds. There is a big resistance to gurus in the West,*

although they are part and parcel of Indian life. Also, when we are asked questions we try to give proper answers and don't pull the shutters down. Our answers create an atmosphere of receptivity. People enjoy the fact that we are peaceful and have a desire to communicate.

NANCY FALK: *What is enormously attractive about the Spiritual University is its consistency, and the fact that they practice what they preach.*

I have encountered many gurus where the guru has a limousine or calls wealthy followers to his room. And to find a group of people who actually live their ideals to the extent the BKs do is quite extraordinary. They have a very deep faith and they operate out of this.

This group is still young, in religious terms, and at its core are a group of people who knew the founder and went through trying times. They have been well and truly tested. I have found that when a religious group encounters great opposition at the time of its founding, this builds a deep bond of commitment between its followers.

Because the BKs spend so much time in meditation, they are enabled to look at their own actions and stand back. The fact that BKs live together in centers means that they are reinforcing and supporting one another. And the fact that they come to Madhuban time and again is a source of renewed commitment.

All the complexes on Mount Abu are peaceful, strong, beautiful places and this allows regrouping. The fact of the lifestyle makes a huge difference as well, and is essential when they live as intensely as they do.

The practice of celibacy—which Westerners find very hard—frees them from conflicting relationships. In ordinary life you can be pulled in so many different directions, and the BKs cut down hard on inessentials.

In the outside world there is great emphasis on competition and divisiveness. The BKs provide a mutually supportive community at their centers, and this is unique, from what I've observed. The BKs are remarkably free of racism and casteism and both these factors are interacting to enable them to carry out their work. In the kitchens, upper-class women are sitting next to village women, and this is very unusual in India, but is consistent with what I've seen in BK centers elsewhere.

It is certainly unusual to find well-to-do people sitting with and working with servants. The fact that women are in charge also contributes to the BK success, I feel.

In India there is the perception that women are more flexible and self-sacrificing than men, and more inclined towards purity. In India women are trained to take a lot, and this gives them power. The more a woman bends and endures, the tougher she becomes. You read about the oppression of women in India, but there should also be an appreciation of their toughness and inner strength.

Women have learned alternative ways of doing things, they have learned to be intuitive. Another secret of the BKs' success is that the Dadis are unusually open to new ideas. As soon as the fax machine came out, they saw its possibilities. The same with e-mail, solar technology, satellite links. There are telephones, mobiles [phones], computers everywhere. Women who have been severely tested pick up these skills, and become inventive and resourceful.

A further point is that people notice that the BKs are not money-grubbing. Gifts are made freely, and this enhances the likelihood of generosity. Because everything is given, there is no waste, no squandering. Much of the expertise comes from BK members, and they are extremely efficient in their use of resources. The excuse of other spiritual groups for high fees is that Westerners only value things they pay for. My experience has been the direct opposite: that those who give spiritual gifts away are respected more. The BKs have no source of generating money or income, and everything comes from contributions.

To sum up, I would put the BKs' success down to four main factors. These are: the power of example; the power of community—the extraordinary welcome everybody is given; attention to detail—lighting, music, landscaping, art; and the power to laugh at oneself. The BKs have a wonderful ability to step back and poke fun at themselves.

SISTER MOHINI, *New York: We have kept our principles. Also, nobody has any wish for status above anybody else. Once, somebody came to Dadiji with some better cloth for her sari. This cloth was very expensive, and the first question Dadiji asked was: Can everybody have one the same? The answer was no, there was not enough money, and so Dadiji kept to the same sari. The question always asked when it comes to having expensive things is: Can everybody have it? If the answer is no, then nobody has it. In Madhuban, everybody eats the same food, and there is no idea of "high table."*

For many years Dadi Janki used to travel economy, as it was impossible to afford business class for everybody. It was only when she became too old and frail to travel economy that she finally succumbed. But not without a great struggle! People like to see that we are genuinely egalitarian in our own set-up.

GAYATRI NARAINE: "We have no dark secrets, and anybody can share the knowledge. This removes the fear factor and as the basis of our teaching is that we are all souls, we cannot discriminate between the worthy and the unworthy. If the truth is kept away from people, they cannot change. In religions of the past, the masses never had access to truth, so they had no way of making informed choices."

DADI PRAKASHMANI: *There are four main reasons for our success. These are:*

1. Establishment of God as the Supreme Father, meaning that there are no gurus.
2. The knowledge given is based on truth. There are specific facts and figures, and no blind faith.
3. Brahma Baba set a practical example of the way we should live.
4. Most importantly, Baba always kept the sisters ahead of himself. In the world, nobody else has ever kept women in front in the same way.

Can you give ten simple tips to maintain peace in every-day situations?

SISTER MEERA (based in Australia):

1. Begin each day with one positive affirmative thought and spend the first ten minutes of each day in meditation.

2. Every morning, feed the intellect with spiritual knowledge. The food we feed the intellect with in the morning is like breakfast for the soul.

3. Take care of the food you eat. Feed the body carefully as food intimately affects the mind.

4. Be aware of the company you keep. We have a slogan: as the company, so the person.

5. Remember "traffic control," the one-second stop. For one minute in every hour, ask yourself the question: Who am I? Where have I come from? Whose child am I? Stay still and the answer will come. This will keep you calm throughout the day.

6. Remember that past is past. Live in the present and don't be anxious about the future.

7. Keep a good balance between the spiritual and the physical life.

8. Don't neglect your responsibilities. Be an optimist. See problems as a challenge and then look for a solution. We are on the field of action but we should maintain spiritual awareness while performing actions.

9. Tell yourself that whatever happened up till now has happened because it had to happen, and that whatever happens tomorrow is for the best.

10. Finish the day winding up the whole day's routine and spend another ten minutes in meditation for the first

month. Then you can increase it to half an hour in the second month. By the third month, you will start to see transformation in your life. This is a simple peace formula, and you should share it with others you meet.

The BKs are clearly a highly successful organization, yet even so the university is not generally well-known. Why is this?

JAYANTI: Why have people heard of certain other so-called spiritual organizations? The answer to that is because of sex and money. Those organizations that do not demand large fees and have no sexual interest for the media have a low profile. Usually, spiritual organizations are only heard of for their misdeeds, not for their good deeds.

What steps are being taken towards modernization of the university?

JAYANTI: The Dadis have given a framework which was received from Brahma Baba. Although he gave the original impetus to the university, he never went out on service himself; that was left to the sisters. Because the senior sisters have remained egoless, they have given the rest of us a lot of freedom to express ideas. The Million Minutes of Peace was such a departure for us, and our other programs and courses, such as Self-Management, Leadership, Positive Thinking, Stress Management and so on, have all happened because of the openness and humility of the Dadis. The thing is, people have come to trust the Dadis, and that is why we can be forward-looking without compromising our original principles.

EPILOGUE

A number of people, BKs and others, have now given their views on why the BKs have become such a successful spiritual organization without ever fund-raising, advertising, mounting recruitment campaigns or trying to capture headlines.

My own view of why the organization appeals to people, even those who may not consider full commitment to all its ideas and beliefs, is that they have an unshakeable set of core principles from which they operate. They then assess every potential new scheme, building, program and event from the perspective of these principles. Before engaging in any new field they apply existing spiritual principles, and if these are met, they then "ask Baba."

The next thing is to meditate on it, and spend much time in silence to ponder the matter. Clarity is the key. Once there is clarity, the scheme can go ahead. If this factor is not present, the idea is put on hold. There is no wishful thinking, no vague hope that something might work out. With this method of checking, once any scheme receives the BK seal of approval, there is total energy and commitment behind it, and nothing is engaged upon half-heartedly.

Dadi Janki also believes that one reason for the BK success in so many different enterprises is that very few BKs have actually been professionals in building, design, public speaking, in the performance arts, in computers and so on. Mostly, they have learned on the job and Dadi believes that this has enabled them to be more humble and less egotistical than they might otherwise be about each project. She said: "All the computer technicians, solar energy experts, lighting experts and so on who worked to make Gyan Sarovar what it is were amateurs." When people are enthusiastic amateurs, they are likely to try harder, and acknowledge that they might have something to learn. And, of course, none of the original Dadis has had any professional training, yet each has emerged as an expert in a certain field: Dadi Prakashmani is a skilled administrator; Dadi Janki is a gifted leader and speaker; other Dadis in Madhuban are efficient organizers of large teams.

In the West, Jayanti has become a world-class interpreter of spiritual matters, and Maureen Goodman has become an innovative and imaginative program organizer and deviser. Manda Patel has discovered an innate skill at running retreats and Jaymini Patel (no relation) runs the literature department efficiently and carefully. Yet none had any previous training for these tasks.

The senior men, too, have played their part. In Madhuban, Nirwair is a talented and artistic designer and instigator of new buildings; Ramesh attends to finances and accounts; Brij Mohan edits publications, and Jagdish, who died in 2001 at age seventy, was the writer.

Another factor is that, although the BKs are now very numerous, they see themselves as one big family. Because of this perception, they come together every single morning, at centers all over the world, to hear exactly the same *murli* as each other. Nobody misses out on this daily ritual, and the morning class is also another important aspect. No ordinary work can begin until *murli* and morning class are over.

It seems that the study they do every day actually works to weaken bad habits and bring out the best in people. Gradually, the hold on attachment, lust, greed, ego and so on is lessened as meditation practice continues. Surya, in charge of catering at Madhuban, said that he realized he had finally conquered lust when he no longer even had dreams about sex and celibacy. It can in some cases take a lot of effort to release oneself from bad habits, but meditation enables it to be an effective and permanent release — eventually.

The fact that the organization is run by women also makes a difference, as it gives the institution a unique quality. Most, if not all, other spiritual groups and religions remain male-dominated and women are still tokens, rather than being central. Although women can now become rabbis and Christian priests, they are still not found heading any of these traditional religions. Almost all Indian gurus are male, and some are extremely arrogant and egotistical.

How important is celibacy? Well, the fact that all dedicated members are celibate means that their energies are not concentrated elsewhere. Because the seniors have no partners and no children, this means their attention is not distracted by the demands of a nuclear family.

The fact that they live an extremely simple lifestyle themselves also means that there are no external distractions. Further, because the organization keeps expanding and trying new things, members don't get bored. There are constant new challenges. The Oxford retreat center, for instance, has set a pattern for other retreat centers, and new programs and courses are being instigated all the time.

Another new departure has been the "Inner Space" shops in busy city areas. These shops offer a meditation experience, classes, programs, courses and literature, and are much used by business and professional people in their lunch hours and after work.

For me, though, the overwhelming reason why I like the BKs is because of their lack of ego and arrogance, and readiness to laugh at themselves. The problem with so many spiritual movements, particularly modern ones, is that they take themselves so deadly seriously, and this can make them unapproachable and aloof. Many New Age movements, too, have no humor in them whatever.

But the Dadis are always ready to laugh and, if you like, to make fools of themselves. Why? Because they are all so remarkably free of ego, and this means they are never self-important, never standing above things. At a garden fête held at Oxford one summer Dadi Janki and Dadi Prakashmani rode round the estate in golf buggies, to the amusement of the onlookers. At a big ceremony celebrating the Indian festival of Holi, where Indians squirt colored water over people they meet, Dadi Gulzar was squirting the gathering with water from a toy water pistol. Their ability to laugh keeps them light and also helps to prevent ego from building up.

The Dadis are all very game. They will meet anybody, talk to anybody, address audiences of all sizes, from gatherings of less than a dozen to several thousands. They are always ready to have their photo taken, to be interviewed, quoted. The fact that they are constantly evaluating and embarking on new challenges keeps them young; as it were, ageless. When you look into the Dadis' eyes you see that they are alive and sparkling, those of a young person.

As the BK life is so very dedicated and disciplined, it is never going to be for everybody. It is very high-minded, very uncompromising in its way, and requires great dedication and application. Much as I like and admire the sisters and brothers, and count many of them among my best friends, I unfortunately remain too attached to my wicked ways (for the moment at least) to be able to surrender myself totally to the organization. Also, I have never had a transcendental meditation experience, which is the main aspect that keeps people going through thick and thin—and there are dark patches, moments of doubt and sorrow, in everybody's spiritual journey. As my former husband Neville remarked: "It's heaven and hell: heaven when you keep your peace of mind; hell when you don't."

But then, such surrender, such clear-eyed commitment, is not everybody's path, and the BKs acknowledge this, which is why they never have recruitment drives or charismatic, seductive gatherings where emotions are manipulated.

Over the years they have worked hard to make their message accessible and relevant to everybody, so that each person can take something, and in this they have succeeded mightily. Nobody can argue with the advice that we should always try to be positive and happy; that we should work hard to rid ourselves of fear; try to remain stable and not let others' negativity affect our own equilibrium, and to be able to see others as brother or sister souls; as equal, not more or less elevated, than ourselves.

The teachings about the cycle, consciousness, karma, the soul and the Supreme Father put these precepts into a neat framework, and enable us to take responsibility for our actions and their consequences.

I have found it useful to act as if the BKs teachings were true, and live my life accordingly.

If I happen to find a better, more logical and exact explanation of where we come from, why we are here and where we are going, then I will take that on board.

So far, though, I haven't.

For me, the BKs remain by far the most genuinely spiritual organization I have ever encountered. Their background is colorful and unusual, and the many projects they have undertaken are original and courageous. I have observed them closely and objectively for very many years and so far, have not found anything wrong. There are no skeletons in the closet and there is no inconsistency in their beliefs.

For all these qualities, they must be unique.

ABOUT THE BRAHMA KUMARIS WORLD SPIRITUAL UNIVERSITY

The Brahma Kumaris World Spiritual University is an international organization working at all levels of society for positive change. Established in 1937 it now carries out a wide range of educational programs for the development of human and spiritual values throughout its 4,000 centers in over seventy countries.

The university is a nongovernmental organization in general consultative status with the Economic and Social Council of the United Nations and in consultative status with UNICEF. It is also the recipient of seven UN Peace Messenger awards.

Locally, centers provide courses and lectures in meditation and positive values, enabling individuals to recognize their true potential and make the most of life.

The university offers all its services free of charge.

Brahma Kumaris World Spiritual University
International Headquarters
Pandav Bhawan, Post Box No. 2, Rajasthan, Mount Abu
307501, India
Tel: (+91) 2974 38261 to 68
Fax: (+91) 2974 38952 / 38883
E-mail: *bkabu@vsnl.com*

International Co-ordinating Office and Regional Office
   for Europe and the Middle East
Global Co-operation House, 65 Pound Lane, NW10 2HH
London United Kingdom
Tel: (+44) 20 8727 3350 • Fax: (+44) 20 8727 3351
E-mail: *london@bkwsu.com* • Web site: *www.bkwsu.org.uk*

Regional Office for Africa
Brahma Kumaris Raja Yoga Centre, (Global Museum for a
Better World), Maua Close, off Parklands Road, Westlands
P.O. Box 123, Sarit Centre, Nairobi, Kenya
Tel: (+254) 2 743 572 / 741239 / 741849
Fax: (+254) 2 743 885
E-mail: *bkwsugm@holidaybazaar.com*

Regional Office for Australia and South East Asia
78 Alt Street, Ashfield, NSW 2131, Sydney, Australia
Tel: (+61) 2 9799 9880 • Fax: (+61) 2 9716 7795
E-mail: *indra@brahmakumaris.com.au*

Regional Office for North, Central and South America and the Caribbean
Global Harmony House, 46 S. Middle Neck Road
Great Neck, NY 11021, United States
Tel (+1) 516 773 0971 • Fax (+1) 516 773 0976
E-mail: *newyork@bkwsu.com* • Web site: *www.ghhny.com*

Regional Office for Russia, CIS and Baltic Countries
2 Gospitalnaya Ploschad, Build. 1, Moscow 111020, Russia
Tel (+7) 095 263 02 47 • Fax: (+7) 095 261 32 24
E-mail: *bkwsu@mail.ru*
Web Site: *www.brahmakumarisru.com*

MAIN CENTERS
CARRIBEAN

87 Kendal Hill Development
Christ Church
St. Michael
Barbados
Tel: (+1) 246 429 2449 • Fax: (+1) 246 228 1245
E-mail: *omo@caribsurf.com*

Raja Yoga Centre
16 Leaders Avenue
P.O. Box 280
Montego Bay
Jamaica
Tel (+1) 876 979 5261 / 971 8197 • Fax: (+1) 876 952 1743
E-mail: *jamaica@bkwsu.com*

55-57 Pointe-a-Pierre Road
San Fernando
Trinidad
Tel (+1) 868 653 9642 • Fax: (+1) 868 657 3741
E-mail: *rajayoga@trinidad.net*

CENTRAL AMERICA

Ap 2306-1000
San Jose
Costa Rica
Tel: 506 256 65 53 • Fax: 506 256 52 27
E-mail: *costarica@bkwsu.com* • Web site: *www.vozdepaz.net*

Av Cementerio
Las Flores 17-33
Zona 7, Col San Ignacio Mixco
Guatemala City
Guatemala
Tel: 502 5945 529 / 5945 614 • Fax: 502 5945 489
E-mail: *guatemala@bkwsu.com*

Cocoteros 172
Col. Nueva Santa María
Mexico City DF 02800
Mexico
Tel: 52 5 556 2152 • Fax: 52 5 556 2468
E-mail: *ombkmex@infosel.net.mx*

SOUTH AMERICA

Santa Fe, 1863-2 Piso
C1123AAA Buenos Aires
Argentina
Tel: 54 11 4815 1811 • Fax: 54 11 4815 1811
E-mail: *argentina@bkwsu.com*

Rua Dona Germaine Burchard 589
05002-062
Sao Paulo / SP
Brazil
Tel: 55 11 3864 3694 / 55 11 3864 2639
Fax: 55 11 3872 7838
Literature Tel: 3873 3304 • Fax: 3673 3836
E-mail: International: *brasil@bkumaris.com.br*
Web site: *www.bkumaris.com.br/*

Pocuro No. 2841
Providencia
Santiago
Chile
Tel: 56 2 223 2062
Fax: 56 2 209 4429
E-mail: *bkumaris@terra.cl*

Diagonal 88 BIS #27-06
Polo Club
Apartado Aereo 90543
Bogota-DC
Colombia
Tel: 57 1 533 1339 • Fax: 57 1 623 4508
E-mail: *bogota@bkcolombia.com*
Web site: *www.bkcolombia.com*

Valle Riestra N 652
San Isidro
Lima
Peru
Tel: 51 1 264 5308
E-mail: *bkperu@qnet.com.pe* • Web site: *www.bkperu.org*

Benito Lamas, 2812
Montevideo
Uruguay
Tel 5982 709 6106
E-mail: *bkumaris@adinet.com.uy*

UK AND IRELAND

Global Co-Operation House
65 Pound Lane
London NW10 2HH
Tel: 0181 727 3350
E-mail: *london@bkwsu.com*

Global Retreat Center, Nuneham Park
Nuneham Courtenay
Oxford OX44 9PG
Tel: 01865 343 551
E-mail: *infoshare@bkwsugrc.demon.co.uk*

8 Haxby Court, Felbridge Close
Atlantic Wharf
Cardiff CF1 2BH
Wales
Tel: 01222 480 557

20 Polwarth Crescent,
Edinburgh EH11 1HW
Scotland
Tel: 0131 229 7220
E-mail: *bkedinburgh@compuserve.com*

36 Lansdowne Road, Ballsbridge
Dublin 4
Ireland
Tel: 353 1 660 3967
E-mail: *bknick@indigo.ie*

USA

Peace Village Learning and Retreat Center
Brahma Kumaris World Spiritual
P.O. Box 99
Haines Falls, NY 12436 - 0099
Tel (+1) 518 589 5000 • Fax: (+1) 518 589 5005
E-mail: *peacevillage@bkwsu.com*
Web site: *www.peacevillage.com*

Brahma Kumaris Meditation Centre and Gallery
306 5th Avenue, 2nd Floor
New York, NY 10001
Tel: (+1) 212 564 9533

United Nations Office
Brahma Kumaris
866 UN Plaza, Suite 436
New York, NY 10017
Tel: (+1) 212 688 1335 • Fax: (+1) 212 504 2798
E-mail: *bkun@bkwsu.com* • Web site: *www.livingvalues.net*

Brahma Kumaris
9913 Georgia Avenue
Silver Spring, MD 20902
Tel: (+1) 301 593 4990 • Fax: (+1) 301 593 4990
E-mail: *washington@bkwsu.com*

1821 Beacon Street, #1
Brookline, MA 02445
Tel: (+1) 617 734 1464 • Fax: (+1) 617 734 7263
E-mail: *boston@bkwsu.com*
Web site: *www.bkwsuboston.com*

5207, 154th Avenue NE
Redmond, WA 98052
Tel: (1) 425 861 6926
Fax: (+1) 425861 6926
E-mail: *seattle@bk.com*

810 Summerwalk Parkway
(off Lawrenceville Highway)
Tucker, GA 30084
Tel: (+1) 770 939 1480 • Fax: (+1) 770 939 8354
E-mail: *atlanta@bkwsu.com*

3525 Country Square Drive
#P 207
Carrollton, TX 75006
Tel: (+1) 972478 7089 • Fax (+1) 972 478 5859
E-mail: *dallasbkwsu@flash.net* • Web site: *www.bktexas.com*

2101 North Lamar #5
Austin, TX 78705
Tel: (+1) 512 789 7685
E-mail: *austin@bkwsu.com* • Web site: *www.bktexas.com*

401 Baker Street
San Francisco, CA 94117
Tel: (+1) 415 563 4459
Fax: (+1) 415 563 4673
E-mail: *bksfo@aol.com*

908 South Stanley Avenue
Los Angeles, CA 90036
Tel: (+1) 323 933 2808
Fax: (+1) 323 933 7376
E-mail: *bkla@pacbell.net*

2428 Griffith Park Boulevard
Los Angeles, LA 90039
Tel: (+1) 323 664 0022
Fax: (+1) 323 664 0022
E-mail: *aglakebks@aol.com*

302 Sixteenth Street
Seal Beach, CA 90740
Tel: (+1) 562 430 4711
Fax: (+1) 562 430 9754
E-mail: *sealbeach@bkwsu.com/diane@livingvalues.net*

4160 S.W. 4th Street
Miami, FL 33134
Tel: (+1) 305 442 2252
Fax: (+1) 305 442 6745
E-mail: *miami@bkwsu.com*

Mind's Eye Museum
2207 E. Busch Boulevard
Tampa, FL 33612
Tel: (+1) 813 935 0736 / Office: 987-2525
Fax: (+1) 813 985 9660
E-mail: *tampa@bkwsu.com*

3221 East Monoa Road
Honolulu, HI 96822
Tel: (+1) 808 988 3141
Fax: (+1) 808 988 1145
E-mail: *hawaiibk@lava.net*

CANADA

897 College Street
Toronto Ontario M6H 1A1
Tel (+1) 416 537 3034
E-mail: *bktoronto@titan.tcn.net*